"Holley Gerth is a fresh voice for every woman—she echoes the voice of our Father."

—**Ann Voskamp**, *New York Times* bestselling author
of *One Thousand Gifts*

"If you need a friend to walk with you through the hard stuff in life, to cheer you on with encouragement, to help you find strength and joy in the midst of life's difficulties—this book is for you! God writes love and assurance on the canvas of hearts through the hands of Holley Gerth. In each chapter you will learn how to hold on to hope, hold on to who you are, and hold on to all God has promised, knowing and believing that no matter what, 'You're going to be okay!'"

—**Renee Swope**, bestselling author of *A Confident Heart;*
Proverbs 31 Ministries radio cohost; speaker; blogger; www.ReneeSwope.com

"*You're Going to Be Okay* is a lifeline for those sinking under waves of pressure and expectation. Holley Gerth speaks bold truth in this must-have book for women who long to be set free and who are desperate to know who they are in Christ and how they can overcome life's struggles. I cannot recommend it highly enough."

—**Emily T. Wierenga**, author of *Chasing Silhouettes*
and *Mom in the Mirror*, www.emilywierenga.com

"When you feel like your life is falling apart all around you—when you really need to know you're going to be okay—the last thing you need is a sermon. What you really need is a friend. And that's what readers will find in Holley Gerth's latest gem of a book. This is more than a book; it's a walk with a trusted friend. Holley's wisdom, authenticity, and warmth resonate on every page. We don't get rote answers with Holley; we get a deep sense of how we are deeply loved by God, who meets us right where we are. *You're Going to Be Okay* is a must-read for anyone who feels like they're not enough. It's a resource for anyone who thinks they can't face another day. It's an important book for anyone who needs to know that God is near. Which means this: *You're Going to Be Okay* is a book for all of us."

—**Jennifer Dukes Lee**, author of *Love Idol*

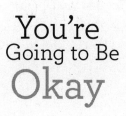

# You're
## Going to Be
# Okay

## Books by Holley Gerth

*You're Already Amazing*

*The "Do What You Can" Plan* (ebook)

*You're Made for a God-Sized Dream*

*Opening the Door to Your God-Sized Dream*

*If We Could Have Coffee . . .* (ebook)

# You're
## Going to Be
# Okay

*Encouraging Truth Your Heart Needs to Hear,*
*Especially on the Hard Days*

*Holley Gerth*

## Revell
**a division of Baker Publishing Group**
**Grand Rapids, Michigan**

Published by Revell
a division of Baker Publishing Group
P.O. Box 6287, Grand Rapids, MI 49516-6287
www.revellbooks.com

Printed in the United States of America

Library of Congress Cataloging-in-Publication Data is on file at the Library of Congress, Washington, DC.

ISBN 978-0-8007-2062-9

Unless otherwise indicated, Scripture quotations are from the Holy Bible, New International Version®. NIV®. Copyright © 1973, 1978, 1984, 2011 by Biblica, Inc.™ Used by permission of Zondervan. All rights reserved worldwide. www.zondervan.com

Scripture quotations labeled ESV are from The Holy Bible, English Standard Version® (ESV®), copyright © 2001 by Crossway, a publishing ministry of Good News Publishers. Used by permission. All rights reserved. ESV Text Edition: 2007

Scripture quotations labeled NKJV are from the New King James Version. Copyright © 1982 by Thomas Nelson, Inc. Used by permission. All rights reserved.

14   15   16   17   18   19   20        7   6   5   4   3   2   1

To Poppi,
Hollie Brookshire,
who has lived well for almost a century.
Thank you for showing me what it means
to choose resilience, joy, and love.

# Contents

# Introduction

If your life isn't perfect, this is for you.

If you've ever been disappointed, this is for you.

If you sometimes have bad hair days, this is for you.

If you've dreamed a big dream and then watched it fall apart, this is for you.

If you are human and live in a fallen world, this is for you.

She tucks her head in her hands for just a moment, then looks up with a sigh. "It's been a tough day," she whispers with a half smile. I nod in agreement and touch her hand with mine. "I just need to know ..." she continues. "I just need to know I'm going to be okay."

Don't we all?

I remember being a newlywed with a husband who was trying to figure out how to help me. He would offer advice and solutions with such good intentions. Finally, I stopped him and said, "This is what I need to hear: just tell me I'm going to be okay."

I hear the same from women all across the world. I've heard it in conversations, in emails, as a life coach, when I've been a speaker, and when I worked as a counselor. We don't want more "how-to" or to be told what to do. When life surprises us, smacks us on the behind, and runs away with our dreams, it's our hearts that are left standing there hurting. Our heads know the truth. We understand what's supposed to make it right in that moment. But somehow even the truth can ring hollow sometimes.

So what do we do then? Is it even possible to live with joy, resilience, and strength in this broken world? After connecting with thousands of women about this topic, searching Scripture, and living my own journey, I can say without reservation: *yes!*

And it's not just possible; *it's what God desires for you.*

Jesus said, "In this world you will have trouble. But take heart! I have overcome the world" (John 16:33).

*Take heart.*

What does that even mean?

That's what we'll explore in these pages. How our hearts can deal with the dog messing up the rug and the devil messing up our lives. How we can face little irritations and life's big tragedies and still thrive. How we can bounce back faster and fall down less. How we can spend more of our time living and less of our time regretting.

Is this easy? Nope. Nothing worthwhile ever is. Research shows that almost half of your happiness can be attributed to one factor: you.[1] How you react to life turns out to be far more important than what life throws at you. When you decide to take charge of your heart, everything changes because *you* change.

This book isn't for victims.

It's not for whiners.

It's not for pessimists or perfectionists.

(And, yes, we've all been all of those, and we can learn to be different.)

It's for people.

Women like you.

Women like me.

You are stronger than you know.

You are loved more than you realize.

You are part of a greater plan, and nothing can stop God's purposes for you.

*You're going to be okay.*

I promise.

And what's even more important: God promises too.

Take heart, friend. Good things are ahead.

# **Who** You Are
# Is Still the Same

Stressed.

Tired.

Depressed.

Anxious.

Frustrated.

Broken.

The labels stick to our hearts, covering our identities until we can't see who we are anymore. We come to believe that our struggles and circumstances define us. But those are just descriptions, not determinations. Who you are doesn't change based on the kind of day, week, or year you have. You are a daughter of God, a holy princess, a woman loved beyond all you can imagine. *No matter what.*

A friend going through a difficult time called me. As we talked, she kept repeating the same phrase: "I guess I'm just the girl who has this struggle." I finally stopped her and said as gently as I could, "That's *where* you're at right now. It's not *who* you are."

You see, life's obstacles are temporary. Who you are is eternal.

My husband and I recently visited Canada for a few days. Imagine if we stepped into a coffee shop, the baristas asked, "Who are you?" and I answered, "I'm a Canadian, y'all." They would take one look at my touristy tennis shoes and listen to my Southern accent, then shake their heads in bemused disagreement. I imagine you would do the same. Because you understand this: there's a difference between a visitor and a citizen. And "our citizenship is in heaven," declares the apostle Paul (Phil. 3:20).

When we look at what's happening in our lives and say, "This is who I am," it's much like me declaring myself a Canadian just because I crossed the border. As my friend and fellow writer Jennifer Dukes Lee recently wrote me in an email, "We don't have to be a 'citizen' of the 'place' we're standing in right now. I'm not a citizen of Sad City, a resident of Rejectionville, or a townsperson of Trouble Town. I have a citizenship in heaven."[1] Your circumstances may change, but who you truly are remains forever the same. Your identity is eternally secure in Christ.

*What are the words you have been using to describe who you are based on where you are in life right now? Write three here (for example,* stressed, divorced, sick, lonely*):*

_____

_____

_____

Whatever you wrote is where you're at, not who you are. It's your current location. To help shift your perspective, rewrite those words as phrases that show they aren't part of your identity. For example, "I'm going through a stressful time right now" or "I have experienced a divorce" or "I'm battling an illness."

_____

_____

_____

Once you know who you're not, it's time to ask God one of the most important questions of all: "Who am I?" Perhaps there's no more important time for seeking these answers than when we're in the middle of a bad day or hard season. We lean into God's heart and ask, "Who am I *in spite of this*? Tell me what's true about me no matter what happens."

I love how Hebrews reassures us, "It is impossible for God to lie" (6:18). Your circumstances will lie to you. Your emotions will lie to you. Even other people will lie to you. But not God. And because of this, "We have this hope as an anchor for the soul, firm and secure" (6:19). Your identity is secure. Nothing going on in your life can change it.

So how does God answer that question? What does he say to us about who we truly are? Let's look at what he says is true of you, no matter what you are going through today.

### You Are Loved

Worrying that our circumstances can separate us from love isn't a new idea. The apostle Paul reassured some of the earliest Christians:

> I am convinced that neither death nor life, neither angels nor demons, neither the present nor the future, nor any powers, neither height nor depth, nor

anything else in all creation, will be able to separate us from the love of God that is in Christ Jesus our Lord. (Rom. 8:38–39)

What the enemy tries to whisper to us whenever we struggle is this: "If God really loved you, this wouldn't be happening." In other words, something is *wrong* with you or everything in your life would be *right*. But we live in a fallen world. We are broken people. All of us face hardships and have obstacles to overcome.

Have you believed this lie?

*I am not really loved.*

If so, then it's time to trade it for the truth.

*I am infinitely loved.*

God's love is so extraordinary that the psalmist declared it to be "as high as the heavens are above the earth" (Ps. 103:11). If you need a reminder, step outside and try to find the end of the sky. That's how much you're loved.

We all hear this lie at different times in our lives. Pause and consider when it impacts you most. For me it's when I have so much on my plate that it feels more like a platter! A few months ago I found myself in an especially busy season. I spoke with my fabulous life coach, Denise Martin, about it. I said, "I feel overwhelmed, and so I must be a failure. And if I'm a failure, then I can't really be loved."

She quickly responded with a question. "Holley, what does being overwhelmed have to do with being a failure or being loved? It just means you're really busy!"

Because I tend to believe that I have to earn love by being productive, when my to-do list doesn't get done, I assume I can't be loved. I hope you're reading this and shaking your head at how silly this sounds. But that's exactly what happens—the moment we call out those inner lies, we can see them for what they really are. As soon as Denise spoke, I knew she was right. I let out a big sigh of relief as I realized God's love for me doesn't change based on what I accomplish. Instead, it's a free gift.

Think about your life. I shared that I often believe love is earned through what I do. What is it for you? Here are some common beliefs about love being conditional:

*If I am perfect, I am loved.* So if I'm not perfect or my life isn't, then I must not be loved.

*If people approve of me, I am loved.* So if someone is upset with me or I let someone down, I must not be loved.

*If I am happy all the time, I am loved.* So if I have a bad day or go through a difficulty, then I must not be loved.

Your turn—fill in the blank: *If I am _____, then I am loved. So if _____, then I must not be loved.*

These false beliefs trap us in a vicious cycle. We try harder and harder to meet the standards so that we're loved. But doing so only leads to exhaustion, which makes it more difficult to try harder, which makes us feel more unloved, and on we go. This is especially true in challenging times because we're desperately looking for a way to make things better. We think if we can fix ourselves, then we can fix our lives. But trouble comes to us all. God doesn't promise a problem-free existence. Instead, he offers unconditional love as a shelter for us even on the most difficult of days. Taking refuge in him requires *receiving* and not striving.

God reduces all of the false phrases above to one simple truth: *If you are mine, you are loved.*

You don't have to earn, prove, or strive for anything. And no matter what comes your way, God's love for you doesn't change. Being loved is not just a circumstance in your life; it is who you are.

Yes, it's true.

*You are loved.*

# You Have a Purpose

Stress makes us shortsighted. Our bodies are wired in such a way that when our fight-or-flight system is triggered, we react. We're not thinking noble thoughts about the meaning of life or world peace. We're just trying to save ourselves. That works well in temporary situations; for example, when a bear comes charging out of the woods at us. The trouble is, many of us live in *chronic stress*. That means the stress reaction becomes a lifestyle, which carries a high cost. It takes a toll on our health as well as our relationships. And it makes us forget that we are on this earth for a purpose. We're here not merely to survive but to accomplish what no one else can.

Before you ever came into being, God had a purpose in mind for you. As he alone watched your body being formed in your mother's womb, he already knew what was ahead. "We are God's handiwork, created in Christ Jesus to do good works, which God prepared in advance for us to do" (Eph. 2:10).

When life comes along and slaps us silly, it can feel as if God's purpose for us has now been cancelled. But nothing can stop his purposes for us. Scripture is full of stories in which people found themselves in difficult circumstances that turned out to be part of God's mysterious plan.

Joseph's brothers sold him into slavery because of their jealousy. Then his master's wife falsely accused him of rape, so he landed in prison. But God acted on his behalf, and he ended up second in command of the whole country, which enabled him to save the lives of God's people during a famine.

Esther got drafted into the royal harem along with hundreds of other women. Taken away from everything she knew, she had one shot to win the king's favor. She did so and became the next queen, which eventually gave her the opportunity to rescue the Jewish people from the plot of a wicked man.

Jesus himself faced death on a cross and what seemed like the ultimate defeat. Instead of being welcomed as Savior, he experienced betrayal, mistreatment, and abandonment. Yet three days later he victoriously and joyfully rose again to rescue us all from death.

*Just because your circumstances are hard doesn't mean God's purpose for you has changed.* Joseph, Esther, and even Jesus could have said, "I must have done something wrong. Look at what's happening to me! I'm going to give up and just hang on until heaven." Instead, each one looked past the present and held on to an eternal perspective.

You have not been sidelined.

You have not been disqualified.

You have not been placed on the bench to wait out the rest of the game.

God's purpose for you *will* prevail. In all of history, no person has ever been able to thwart God's ultimate plan. He isn't shocked by the brokenness of this world or even our personal failures. He can redeem and reroute as much as is needed to get us to the destination he has in mind.

Don't let the enemy lie to you, sister. You have a purpose. Right here, right now. In the middle of all of this. You don't have to wait for things to get better. You don't have to wait until you get your act together. You don't have to wait until heaven to experience "life to the full" (see John 10:10).

At this point, some of you may want to throw this book across the room. If so, that's totally fine. Just try not to hit anything breakable.

Those emotions come because life's hard times make us tired. And when we're tired, having a big ol' purpose can feel more like a burden than an opportunity. If you feel that way, tell God. Tell him you're tired. Tell him you're mad. Tell him you don't even really want to do anything worthwhile right now. Then ask him to accomplish his purpose through you anyway.

That's the secret: we don't have to carry the load of living with purpose. We can embrace it, celebrate it, cling to it—but we don't have to make it happen. Proverbs 19:21 says, "Many are the plans in a person's heart, but it is the LORD's purpose that prevails." Our role is simply to be willing, to open our hands and hearts and say, "God, I'm a mess. My life's a mess. I don't even have a clue what I'm doing. But I'm yours. Thank you for creating me with a purpose. Thank you that nothing and no one can destroy that purpose. Use me."

You are valuable, my friend. Of great worth. God is going to use you in unexpected, powerful ways.

*You have a purpose.*

## You Are Irreplaceable

A popular commercial shows a woman approaching a display of the Crown Jewels in a museum. She asks the museum worker to tell her how much they cost because she'd like to buy them. He insists, "They're not for sale, ma'am," to which she replies, "I'm not trying to haggle with you. Just shoot me a number." What she doesn't understand is that the Crown Jewels are priceless because they are irreplaceable. They're not mass-produced. They're one of a kind. So are you.

As I write this, over seven billion people inhabit our planet. But there is only one you. And for as long as the world continues to exist, that will remain true. God doesn't have a plan B for your life. He doesn't have a backup plan for the gifts he's placed within you. You're our one-shot wonder at getting you.

When we're stressed or going through a difficult time, we can quickly lose sight of our worth. We feel small, unseen, incapable, and of little value. It seems everyone else is doing better, has more, or is really making a difference. But not us. We withdraw and start believing we don't have anything to contribute—at least not until things are better in our lives.

But there is only one answer to the question, "When and where does God want to use me?" and it's always, "Right now, right here."

You may think you have nothing to offer. You may want to run and hide. You may tell yourself, "I'll only be in the way." But still God asks, quietly and persistently, "Will you let me use you, right here and right now?"

Your weaknesses and struggles are not reasons for him to give up on you. Instead, they're opportunities for you to show his strength in ways you simply can't on your best days. The apostle Paul wrestled with a "thorn in his flesh" (see 2 Cor. 12:7). We don't know what it was exactly, only that it was an ongoing source of difficulty for him. He begged God to take it away, and many of us are familiar with the divine response. God said, "My strength is made perfect in weakness" (2 Cor. 12:9 NKJV).

In other words, the very places and times when you feel God can use you least are when he may actually shine through you most.

For those of us (like me) who thrive on feeling capable and as if we have something to contribute, this can be hard to take. For much of our lives we may have lived with a feeling of pride over what we could do, what we could offer. Or at least those things provided us with a sense of security. Then we find ourselves stripped bare. When God uses us in those moments, it's humbling because we realize *it never really has been about us*. At first we're offended. Maybe even a little ticked off. All this time we've worked so hard, and God can use us when we feel as if we have nothing to offer at all? Yep. And hopefully, that initial shock leads to a new sense of freedom. We can stop our striving. We can give up working so crazy hard to change the world. We can release our expectations and instead open our hands as well as our plans to God.

............

Here is why you are irreplaceable: because you are made in the image of the God who created the universe, and there is a part of who he is that gets shown only through who you are. Sometimes that happens through our strengths. But sometimes it's through our cracks that his light shines the brightest. On your hardest days and in your best moments, it's still all about him.

Breathe out a big sigh of relief and surrender. Offer yourself to God and say, "Lord, I don't know what I have to give right now. I feel empty. I feel broken. I feel weak. But you are in me now just as you are in the times when I feel the strongest and most capable. I want the world to receive what you have designed me to share. I yield myself to you. Use what little I have to make much of you."

*You are irreplaceable.*

## You Are an Overcomer

Her shoulders slump as she slides into a chair in my counseling office. Her eyes and face speak volumes before she ever says a word. "I feel defeated," she whispers. I nod. It's understandable. The battles she's faced. The way she's fought. The war waging in her world.

I dare to smile just a bit and say, "You may have lost some skirmishes, but that's not who you are. You're still an overcomer." She leans forward, smiles back, shakes a little of the tension off her shoulders. She looks stronger already.

When we have a weak moment, a bad day, a tough year, the enemy of our souls taunts us. "You've lost," he hisses. But that isn't true. The reality is, *we can't lose.*

> Who will bring any charge against those whom God has chosen? It is God who justifies. Who then is the one

who condemns? No one. Christ Jesus who died—more than that, who was raised to life—is at the right hand of God and is also interceding for us. Who shall separate us from the love of Christ? Shall trouble or hardship or persecution or famine or nakedness or danger or sword? As it is written: "For your sake we face death all day long; we are considered as sheep to be slaughtered." No, in all these things we are more than conquerors through him who loved us. (Rom. 8:33–37)

Oh, we get knocked around in this life. We have bumps and bruises. Even our Savior left this world with scars. But that doesn't mean we're defeated. This matters because it changes how we fight. Imagine being a soldier who's going into battle. Your commander tells you, "We have already won. All you have to do today is go in there and obey my commands. Victory is sure." You would fight with less fear and more faith, less hesitancy and more certainty, less regret and more intensity. This is what's true of us.

Even when the disease returns.

Even when our spouse decides not to stay.

Even when we relapse after promising we won't ever again.

I don't say that lightly—oh, how those blows hurt. We ache. We feel the pain. We are human, and that is inescapable. Yet we don't have to let our wounds define us. Like we talked about before, *what happens to us is not who we are.* Even in those moments and circumstances, our identity remains secure.

*What has happened to you that has made you feel defeated?*

---

---

---

Now add God's perspective to what you listed above.

*In all these things, even in* _____
*(write what you shared above here), I am more than a conqueror*
*through him who loved me.*

Defeat is not your destiny. You belong to the One who overcame
even death, and that means there is nothing too difficult for him.
It also means you can't make him lose. Read those words again
slowly: *you can't make him lose.* That matters because the danger
of feeling defeated is the shame that comes with it. Have you ever
heard these thoughts slip through your mind?

*You've let God down.*

*You should be ashamed of yourself.*

*How can you not be doing better by now?*

Those are the sinister whispers of defeat. And they are lies.
God's victory in this world does not depend on you. It depends
on one thing alone: Christ's death on the cross and resurrection
three days later. You can't lose the war for God or for yourself.
It's not about you or me at all. We simply get to partake in the
victory. That means there is no shame in losing a battle now and
then. It simply means we are imperfect people in a broken world.

Finally, be strong in the Lord and in his mighty power.
Put on the full armor of God, so that you can take your
stand against the devil's schemes. For our struggle
is not against flesh and blood, but against the rulers,
against the authorities, against the powers of this dark
world and against the spiritual forces of evil in the
heavenly realms. *Therefore put on the full armor of
God, so that when the day of evil comes, you may be
able to stand your ground, and after you have done
everything, to stand.* Stand firm then, with the belt of
truth buckled around your waist, with the breastplate

of righteousness in place, and with your feet fitted with the readiness that comes from the gospel of peace. In addition to all this, take up the shield of faith, with which you can extinguish all the flaming arrows of the evil one. Take the helmet of salvation and the sword of the Spirit, which is the word of God. (Eph. 6:10–17, emphasis added)

You may have skimmed the passage above (confession: I sometimes do that), but I want you to at least go back and read the words in italics. What we are called to do is simply this: to stand. Not to conquer the world. Not to be the greatest warrior ever. Not to never feel weak or afraid. *Just stand.*

Stand on God's promises.

Stand on faith.

Stand on the hope that victory is sure.

You have already won. You can't be defeated by anything in this life or the next.

*You are an overcomer.*

## You Are Enough

I oversleep again. And a voice whispers, "What's wrong with you?"

I snap at my innocent husband as he pours his cereal. And a voice whispers, "What's wrong with you?"

I let down a friend. I don't finish a project. I forget to feed the dog on time. And I hear again and again, "What's wrong with you?"

I slip into bed that night with a sigh, pull the covers over my head, and close the day with this question: "What's wrong with me?"

When we fail, struggle, or face obstacles, it can make us feel we are not enough. Surely we must somehow be inadequate or this wouldn't be happening. If only we could be stronger, do more, get better, then things would be okay. *We* would be okay. We become the judge and find ourselves lacking.

Are we enough?

There are two answers to this question.

The first is, of course not. We're frail. We're human. We fail. None of us is perfect.

But because of what God has done for us, because of Christ who died for us, because of the Spirit within us, that's not the final answer.

The second and truest answer is, yes, we are enough and so much more.

I shared this story in my first book, *You're Already Amazing*:

> "Lord," I asked, "why do women feel as if we're not enough?"
>
> It seemed I heard a whisper in response: *"Because they're not."*
>
> For a moment I thought I had some holy static happening.
>
> "Excuse me, God, it sounded like you said we're not enough. Could you repeat that, pretty please?"
>
> Again, gently and firmly, "You are not enough."
>
> By then I started thinking perhaps my heart had dialed the wrong number and the devil was on the line. But in that pause it seemed God finished the sentence: "You are not enough . . . *in me you are so much more.*"

- We are *much more* than pretty . . . we are wonderfully made.
- We are *much more* than likeable . . . we are deeply loved.
- We are *much more* than okay . . . we are daughters of the King.

I think the enemy tricks us into believing we are not enough because he knows if we discover the truth, we'll be unstoppable.[2]

More than anything else, the lie that we're not enough is what trips women up when we struggle. I've seen it happen again and again as a life coach and counselor as well as in my own life. The reason is that *as long as we believe we're not enough, we also believe we have to make up for it.* So instead of running to Jesus, we flee to self-improvement, trying harder, exhausting ourselves. But there is a better way. *Receiving.* Letting God fill up our "not enough" with his infinite love, grace, and strength until we're overflowing. "His divine power has given us everything we need for a godly life through our knowledge of him who called us by his own glory and goodness" (2 Pet. 1:3).

In Christ, we have everything we need. We are all we need to be. We are rescued from ourselves and from that question that haunts us, "What's wrong with me?" Instead, we can ask, "Who's within me?" The answer is an infinite God who knows no limits, who hung the stars in place, who hears our every prayer and directs our every step. He offers a fullness that can't be taken away by bad days, weak moments, or even life's greatest tragedies. Yes, we grieve. Yes, we face loss. Yes, we let people down and let people go. But in all of this, who we are is not diminished because the One within us can't be diminished. That never changes, no matter what.

*You are enough.*

## Hold Tight to Who You Are

When we face hard times, bad days, and stress, we see the immediate dangers like lost time and sleep. But the greatest risk can be harder to recognize: losing our identities. Who we are can be covered by our circumstances until the challenges we're facing are all we can focus on when we look in the mirror.

You are not what happens to you.

You are not where you are right now.

You are not your weakest moments or biggest struggles.

Can I lean in and whisper that to you? Oh, friend, I'm praying with all my heart right now as I type these words that you believe it.

You are loved.

You have a purpose.

You are irreplaceable.

You are an overcomer.

You are enough.

This is what's true of you—no matter what your day holds. Don't let your circumstances define you. Instead, hold on to who you really are. To what God whispers to you. To the identity he's given you that's eternally unchanging.

You are who he says you are.

And you are *his*—forever.

# 2

## You're **Stronger** Than You Know

The sound of screeching tires grabs the attention of two moms in a neighborhood. Donna and Abigail run out to discover a child pinned by a car. Without even thinking, they rush to the side of the vehicle and lift it. All 1.1 tons of it. The boy is rescued and makes a full recovery.[1]

We've all heard stories like these—ordinary people discovering superhuman strength when it's needed most. There's something about stress and crisis that brings us to a decision point. Either we're crushed beneath their weight or we suddenly find within ourselves more strength than we knew we possessed. If you're reading these pages, then I'm betting the second is true of you. And even if you don't feel like it is at this moment, it can be. This is the strength you have working within you: "That power is the same as the mighty strength he exerted when he raised Christ from the dead and seated him at his right hand in the heavenly realms" (Eph. 1:19–20).

The strength within you is the same one that raised Christ from the dead! Whew. What does that mean for each of us? It means *God will give us the strength we need to accomplish his purpose in our lives regardless of the circumstances.* Being raised from the dead and seated in the heavenly realms is not on your to-do list in the same way it was for Christ. So God's power is not going to be displayed that way through you. But it means that whatever he does have for you to accomplish, even on the tough days, you can.

What I love about how God works is that there are always two parts: universal and personal. Universal means it applies to everyone who believes in him. So the verse above tells us we all have access to the same power source. Yet God is also infinitely personal, which means the way those universal truths unfold in our lives is unique and different for each one of us. How God's power and strength show in you will never be duplicated by anyone else.

## Your Strengths

When we face stress or bad hair days or the dog eats our homework, the last things on our mind are our strengths. We can name off our weaknesses one after another. But ask us what's going well in the chaos and we're more likely to roll our eyes than give an insightful answer.

But the reality is, you are lifting a car somehow today. I know that because you are here, still moving forward, and asking God to help you. You are stronger than you know.

So in the middle of whatever is going on right now, I want you to pause and take a deep breath as well as a close look at your life. In *You're Already Amazing*, we talked about our core strengths—certain characteristics that are part of our identities throughout our lives. I believe we also have *circumstantial strengths*. In other words, certain parts of us show up when the going gets tough that we didn't even know existed. They're often as much of a surprise to us as they are to those around us. God gives these strengths through his power when we need them. And thankfully, that's not all the time.

### *Circumstantial Strengths*

Circle at least one strength you've shown in a difficult situation:

| | | |
|---|---|---|
| ◦ Adaptable | ◦ Feisty | ◦ Obedient |
| ◦ Authentic | ◦ Flexible | ◦ Optimistic |
| ◦ Believing | ◦ Forgiving | ◦ Organized |
| ◦ Bold | ◦ Funny | ◦ Patient |
| ◦ Brave | ◦ Genuine | ◦ Peaceful |
| ◦ Compassionate | ◦ Gracious | ◦ Persevering |
| ◦ Considerate | ◦ Grateful | ◦ Prayerful |
| ◦ Content | ◦ Helpful | ◦ Resilient |
| ◦ Courageous | ◦ Honest | ◦ Resourceful |
| ◦ Creative | ◦ Hopeful | ◦ Sensitive |
| ◦ Determined | ◦ Humble | ◦ Spirit-led |
| ◦ Disciplined | ◦ Insightful | ◦ Steady |
| ◦ Empathetic | ◦ Joyful | ◦ Tenacious |
| ◦ Encouraging | ◦ Kind | ◦ Trusting |
| ◦ Expressive | ◦ Loving | ◦ Wise |
| ◦ Faith-filled | ◦ Mature | ◦ *Add yours here . . .* |

Which strengths we display and how we display them will depend on what we're facing and God's purposes for us in it. Think of a time in your life when you faced a challenge and someone asked, "How can you be so _____ with so much going on?" That's circumstantial strength. It's possible only through God's power at work in us.

............

Of course, we won't always be strong. Sometimes we'll blow it. Sometimes we'll have a meltdown that makes even the dog worry. Sometimes we'll do the exact opposite of what's best.

And as we say in the South, *honey, it will be all right*. It turns out letting God's strength flow through us takes some practice. The apostle Paul said, "*I have learned* the secret of being content in any and every situation, whether well fed or hungry, whether living in plenty or in want. I can do all this *through him who gives me strength*" (Phil. 4:12–13, emphasis added).

What did Paul need to accomplish God's purpose for his life? Contentment. And how did that happen? Learning.

That means trial-and-error, goof-up-and-ask-forgiveness, give-it-another-shot learning. If Paul needed that process, so do we.

I remember one incident in particular when I royally showed off my ability to get in my own way. I came home from traveling to an event and felt completely exhausted—emotionally and physically. Instead of getting some rest and eating a decent dinner, I did the exact opposite. Then I fussed at my husband. On and on my poor choices went until I ended up bawling in the bathtub. Even my little beagle-basset stood at the door and wondered what in the world was happening. If you could have heard the dialogue in my mind, it would have sounded something like this: "I'm such a bad wife. I'm such a bad friend. I'm such a bad dog owner. Nobody likes me. Everybody hates me. I'll just go eat worms."

Eventually my kind (and very brave) husband tucked me into bed. The next morning when I woke up I couldn't believe how much of a downward spiral I'd let myself get into that day. Sure, I'd had a stressful conference and felt weary. But I added a lot to my own difficulties by the choices I made. I prayed back through the day and asked God what I could do differently next time. I asked my husband to forgive me. I gave the dog an extra bone.

Then I started the day and tried again.

Because that's how it goes in this life.

Pause and think for a moment about the last time you let yourself slip into a downward spiral. What led to it? If you could go back, what would you do differently? What circumstantial strengths would you ask God to give you instead? Reflecting back is part of learning. Sometimes we get so busy, especially when we're stressed, that we simply move on to the next thing. Then we repeat the same mistakes over and over. In other words, we don't learn.

But reflecting is not about beating yourself up. That's called *condemning*, and "there is now no condemnation for those who are in Christ Jesus" (Rom. 8:1). Before you reflect, make a commitment to do so with grace and ask God to help you see the situation through his eyes. He teaches us through truth in love, not condemnation.

Even on your worst days, it's also important to find even one little tiny thing you did right. And there is one, I promise. On my terrible-horrible-no-good-very-bad-day, I retreated to the bathtub, which got me away from anyone who could be slapped around by my loose tongue. I used my circumstantial strength of being *insightful* to say, "Hey, I'm getting out of control. I've got to take a break before I do more damage." I'm sure that nudging came from the Holy Spirit, and I'm so glad I listened. It makes my tummy twist in knots to think how bad things could have gotten had I kept on my current path.

*What about you? Think again to your last hard day. What is one thing you did well despite everything that was going on? Write it here:*

What you wrote above is part of learning too. We don't just want to avoid our mistakes; we also want to recognize and expand whatever we managed to do well in that situation. Every time you recognize a strength, it becomes easier to repeat it. Ask God to show you how his power flows through you—even in your weakest moments. That's how we get stronger.

## Your Stash

A popular cartoon featured Inspector Gadget, a crime-solver who had an endless array of tools at his beck and call. Most of them seemed to reside inside his trench coat. If Inspector Gadget had been on the scene when Donna and Abigail rescued the child from beneath the car, he would have no doubt said, "Go, go gadget car lifter!" and exactly what was needed would have appeared.

Like many other kids, I was fascinated by Inspector Gadget. What would it be like, I wondered, to have everything you need at your fingertips?

In some ways, we're spiritually not that different from that quirky cartoon character. We've been told that "God will meet all your needs" (Phil. 4:19). In other words, we each have a "stash" given to us by God that we can draw on, especially when times get tough. Our strengths are *internal*, whereas our stash is *external*.

Our stash includes anything that helps us accomplish God's purpose for our lives. It can include experiences, education, relationships, and much more.

When stress and bad days hit, we're designed to reach out for the help we need. But our natural tendency is to withdraw instead. We shut down, hole up, limit ourselves to our own little worlds. There's a time and a place for doing so—like when I fled to the bathtub for some damage control. But that response is always meant to be temporary.

The desire to isolate ourselves goes all the way back to the Garden of Eden. Eve and Adam ate the forbidden fruit. Shame overtook them, and they hid. Essentially, they cut themselves off from the relationships and resources given to them by God. But God didn't let them stay in that position. He came looking for them. He drew them back out. And he still does the same for us today.

When we face stress or challenges, whether because of poor choices like Adam and Eve or circumstances beyond our control, we can quickly lose touch with what God has given us. We feel like we have nothing. Everything fades away, and all we can see is the trouble right in front of us.

So once again, let's take another deep breath and a closer look at what's part of your God-given "stash."

## People

Who supports you when life gets stressful? If not many names come to mind, then you're in good company. A study reported in *USA Today* found that half of Americans have two or fewer people to confide in about important things, including friends and family.[2] If you have anyone at all, then you're doing well. If you don't, resist the urge to beat yourself up about it. Life circumstances like moves, divorce, or extended illness can make relationships challenging. Be certain of this—God does want you to have human support. Ask him to send you what you need through other people. Even if it's not as soon as you might like, he will answer.

The first people who come to mind are usually those closest to us: spouses and family members. But sometimes those who are best at supporting us in down times are not the same as those who are in our lives the rest of the time. Who in your life is consistently a comfort and encouragement to you? We may not like to admit it, but sometimes those we love most can actually add to the stress. In that case, we need different sources to go to at times. This might be a mentor, a counselor, a sister in Christ who has the spiritual gift of encouragement, or someone else who may not pop into your mind right away.

Also, it's important to *be* that kind of person for others. Who do you support? Who do you encourage? Those are the people who will likely want to do the same for you. It can be humbling to ask for help, but now is the time to do it. Letting others give to you is a blessing to them as well.

*Who supports and encourages you in stressful times? (Write at least one name below.)*

---

---

## Education and Experiences

As the old saying goes, "you weren't born yesterday," so you've had enough time on this planet to gain some education and experiences. Sometimes education happens in a classroom, but it just as often happens in the school of life. So this is not about your GPA or the degrees you have; instead, it's about what you've learned along the way. Experiences are how you've applied what you've learned. They're the "hands on" aspect of your education.

We can overlook these aspects or dismiss them as not as spiritual. But when we investigate Scripture, we find that God is always intentional even about these details. For example, Pharaoh's daughter raised Moses. He grew up in a palace—the same palace he would one day return to when God called him to deliver the

Israelites. He also spent time in the wilderness as a shepherd before God made him shepherd over a nation as they traveled to the Promised Land. At the time, being raised in a royal household and taking care of sheep might have seemed unimportant to Moses. But surely as he came to fully realize his calling, he could also see just how meaningful the education and experiences he received turned out to be.

Sometimes what we see as wasted time is actually the training ground for what God has in store for us. The lessons we learn and the obstacles we overcome are preparation. Even the rocks you're struggling to climb over today may be the stepping-stones of tomorrow. God never wastes anything. There is great value in where he has led you. And even if you have strayed from his path at times, he's a Redeemer who can transform those mistakes into future benefits to you as well.

*Education: What's one lesson you've learned in life that would be helpful to you now?*

........................................................................................

........................................................................................

*Experience: What's something you have gone through in life that can help you with the stress and circumstances you're facing today?*

........................................................................................

........................................................................................

........................................................................................

Whatever you're going through now is adding to your stash for tomorrow too. Right now it may just feel like frustration and heartbreak. But God won't let this hurt or hard time go unused. The only difference between a lump of coal and a diamond is time and a lot of pressure. What seems worthless now may become a source of great treasure in your stash later.

## God Himself

It's remarkable to consider that the God of the universe is in your stash too. He has declared that he is for you. Everything else you have is from him as well. But like with Jesus on the cross, the greatest gift he always offers is himself.

When it comes to God, we tend to have vague, big-picture ideas about who he is. But as we look closer, we find he reveals himself in deeply personal ways. In particular, the different names that describe him throughout Scripture are also promises about his character. Which one of these speaks most powerfully to you right now?

*El Roi (The God Who Sees, Gen. 16)*—We discover this name of God through the story of Hagar. God promised Abram (later called Abraham) that he would have a son. When God's timing and the impatience of Abram's wife, Sarai, didn't line up, Sarai crafted another plan. Hagar was Sarai's servant, and so Sarai gave Hagar to Abram to sleep with instead. Hagar conceived, but Sarai began to mistreat Hagar, and she fled the household. Alone in the desert, pregnant, Hagar seemed to be in a hopeless situation. She was utterly alone. But then God spoke to her and revealed himself as El Roi, "the God who sees."

When stress comes into our lives, one of the most difficult parts can be feeling as if no one really sees. They don't see the endless diapers we change. They don't see the projects stacked high on our desks. They don't see the X-ray that says the cancer has spread. But there is One who promises his eyes are upon us. Even when we are in the desert and without hope, God sees. And it's not just that he notices—it's that *he knows us*. Deeply, intimately, completely.

*God, today I need you to see . . .*

_____

_____

*Jehovah-Jireh (The Lord Will Provide, Gen. 22)*—Despite the detour with Hagar, God's word to Abraham does eventually come true. With a new name and a new child, it seems all is finally well in the world of this patriarch. But one day God has a strange request: "Sacrifice your son." You can imagine what must have gone through Abraham's mind. "This son? The one you promised? The one we waited for?" Ultimately, Abraham prepares to obey, and then God steps in to provide a ram in Isaac's place. In joy and relief, Abraham names the place "The Lord Will Provide." Looking back on this story, we can easily see that God was giving a preview of how Christ would die for all of us in our place. But Abraham didn't have that viewpoint. All he knew was he felt a desperate need, and God answered.

Need is ultimately a lack of something—time, money, resources, hope, a cure, relationships. Every challenge we face is ultimately about need in some way. God promises to provide for all our needs. Does this mean it will happen in the timing we want? Nope. In the way we want? Nope. But we can trust that God will provide—not just because he can but because it's *who he is.*

*God, today I need you to provide . . .*

_____

_____

*Jehovah Rapha (The Lord Who Heals, Exod. 15:22-27)*—Fast-forward in the history of the people of Israel. As promised, God has turned Abraham's descendants into a mighty nation. Due to a famine, they end up in Egypt and eventually become slaves until God sends Moses to rescue them. During the following forty years they spend in the wilderness, God tests them, provides for them, and teaches them. He also declares, "I am the LORD, who heals you" (Exod. 15:26). We see this even more fully through Christ who died on our behalf, as "by his wounds we are healed" (Isa. 53:5).

The deserts in our lives are the places where we feel we have nothing. It may be in a particular situation. Author Kristen Welch describes getting ready to speak and calling her husband to tell him that she has nothing more to give. He reassures her with words and prayers that God will supply. She completes her speaking engagement and says, "It was in my emptiness that he moved. He encouraged through my brokenness. He asked for my all and my nothing was enough."[3] God healed Kristen's confidence by enabling her to place her security in him. Your desert might be a broken relationship, a physical illness, a lost job, a prodigal child, or an act of rebellion that still has consequences. Whatever it is, God knows this: Yes, we need provision in the desert. But we also need healing for the barren places of our souls.

*God, today I need you to heal . . .*

_____

_____

*Jehovah Shalom (The Lord Is Peace, Judg. 6)*—Even after God brought the Israelites into the Promised Land, their hearts strayed. As a result, they faced oppression from a group of neighboring people called the Midianites. Once again God heard their cries for deliverance, and he appeared to Gideon. I love how this story goes down. Gideon was basically hiding out when the Lord spoke to him. Then he told God his status was so low that he didn't see how he could be of much help. Finally, he asked God to give him not one but three signs to confirm the message. (If Gideon were alive today, he'd be diagnosed with generalized anxiety disorder.) God in his graciousness used Gideon anyway. Gideon built an altar to honor the Lord and named it "The LORD Is Peace" (Judg. 6:24). And peace was what anxious Gideon needed most.

While external circumstances may be difficult, it's the inner turmoil that often wears us down most. We worry. We fret. We lie in bed and stare at the ceiling (at least I do). We think if things were only different, we wouldn't be so uptight. But then when things change, the worry stays—we just switch the focus. What God offers instead is peace. The kind that stays with us no matter what.

Author Ann Voskamp shares how she went away on a retreat in the hopes of discovering peace, but her anxious thoughts only followed her there. What she found instead is that "peace is a person" and he is always there with us ... in the quiet *and* the chaos.⁴ Gideon found out the same. The characteristic of the Lord that stood out to him most was the one his heart most desperately needed: peace.

*God, today I need you to be my peace in* . . .

---

---

*Jehovah Shammah (The Lord Is There, Ezek. 48:35)*—Even after seeing God's hand again and again, the Israelites continued to rebel and were eventually taken into captivity. Still God spoke words of hope through the prophets, including Ezekiel. In one passage, Ezekiel described the heavenly city where we will one day dwell with God. He said simply that the name of the city will be "The LORD Is There" (Ezek. 48:35). The people had lost their Promised Land. They were grieving. Yet in the middle of their tears, God offered this comfort: *That earthly land was never your final destination. You are made for eternity with me.*

Whatever our circumstances are now, our destiny is the same. We will one day be with Jesus forever if we have a personal relationship with him. If you're not sure that you do, you can change that right now. Simply stop and pray, "Lord, I know I am a sinner. I need your forgiveness. Thank you for your death on the cross. I know that is the only way I can be made right with you. No matter what has come before in my life, I now give myself fully and completely to you. Amen." Then find some folks who will help you take the next steps in your journey with Jesus.

If you've drifted from your relationship with him, you can ask for forgiveness and tell him once more that he is Lord of your life.

Because of Jesus, we have hope that whatever we face will not last forever. We can look ahead and know this is certain about our future: the Lord is there.

*God, today I need your perspective on . . .*

_____

_____

The five names for God above are just a start. You can find out more through Scripture and books such as *Lord, I Want to Know You* by Kay Arthur. I read this book in college, and it remains one of the most impactful books in my spiritual journey.

Perhaps the description of God I love most is the one he shares with Moses when he first calls him to lead the Israelites out of Egypt. Moses asks who he should say sent him. God answers with the name "I AM." (Exod. 3:14).

I AM is present tense.

I AM is here with us.

I AM is whatever we need.

I AM is a person.

I AM is personal.

I AM is the answer to our hearts' deepest questions.

*I AM is in your stash.*

God faithfully revealed himself to his people throughout Scripture, and he still does so today.

*God, I need to know who you are for me right now . . .*

---

## What You Have Going for You

Stress and bad days seem to empty our hearts and our hands. We think, "I've got nothing . . . or at least very little." But the reality is, you still have a lot going for you. You have circumstantial strengths that become part of who you are through God's power when you need them. And you have a stash that includes your education, your experiences, and most of all a God who loves you and promises to see you through even the toughest times.

When life presses in on us, we can lose sight of all these things. Sometimes it helps to ask someone you trust, "What do I have going for me?" You might be surprised by the answer. It could be your great sense of humor. The way you faithfully pray. Even that your new hairstyle looks fabulous on you. Whatever the answer, big or small, the real point is to begin to shift your perspective.

Is this easy? No, ma'am. Is it annoying? Um, yes, sometimes. You see, we're all wired with a negativity bias. It's God's way of keeping us out of trouble. For example, we're quicker to see the scary spider on the wall than the lovely photo beside it. That serves us well when it comes to surviving, but not always when it comes to thriving. There's a reason God says we're to be transformed by the renewing of our minds (see Rom. 12:2). It's a process that takes practice. We'll talk more about this later, but for now just know that if looking for your strengths and stash seems a bit tricky or uncomfortable right now, you're in good company. Just keep at it, girl.

One benefit of learning to see your circumstances and self in a different light is that it trains you to do the same for others. You can learn to come alongside others and help them see their strengths and stash in tough moments too. This is best done through encouragement and asking questions. It's about helping others discover the truth their hearts need—just like we've done together.

You have a lot going for you. Even more than you know or can see right now. And you have a great big God who's behind you, beside you, and ahead of you too.

I'm right here as well, cheering you on all the way.

(Disclaimer: I was never coordinated enough to be a cheerleader. I still run into my own coffee table. But I'm making up for it now by occasionally using words as pom-poms. Much safer for everyone.)

# 3

# Your **Mind**
# Is a Powerful Gift

We live with two sets of realities. One flows from the world around us. It's made up of what we can see, taste, touch, smell, and hear. The other one flows from our hearts and minds. It's internal, invisible, but most often even more influential.

We can feel left out even when we're deeply loved. We can feel lonely even when we're surrounded by people. We can feel that we have no hope even when the sun is already beginning to peek through the clouds again. We can feel like we're worth nothing when God sent Jesus to tell us we're worth everything.

It's up to us to choose which reality we live in from day to day. We can focus on what's true or simply believe what we perceive. My friend and fellow writer Lisa-Jo Baker gives this example of how we can choose to act by faith regardless of how we may feel:

> Blink.
> Blink and see it's a mirage.

> *The illusion that there's an inner circle we've been left out of; the lie that we've been left out on purpose.*
>
> We're built for friendship, yes. We have community in our bones. And when we're desperate and blinded by the taunting mirage of the inner circle we will drink the sand—angry, gritty, bitter, and confused.
>
> We can fight to find a way in or we can love on the women where we're at.
>
> *We can obsess over who didn't talk to us or we can focus on the woman we're talking to.*
>
> We can keep looking for a seat at a more popular table or we can pass the bread basket and an introduction to the women sitting right where we already are.[1]

We don't have to wait for our circumstances to change to believe what's true. Hundreds of people don't have to pick up the phone and call to tell us that we're not left out. We don't have to get invited to ten parties. We don't have to win the lottery or be voted most likely to succeed. We can simply listen to the whispers of Jesus telling us what's realer than real and believe it.

## Changing Your Perspective

Jesus said, "Your eye is the lamp of your body. When your eyes are healthy, your whole body also is full of light. But when they are unhealthy, your body also is full of darkness" (Luke 11:34). For years I couldn't understand what that verse meant. Eyes? Lamps? What in the world was Jesus trying to say? Then I finally understood: our perception affects everything. What enables us to truly see the way we're intended? A mind that's filled with light, which means thoughts that line up with truth.

It's interesting to note that in Scripture it's often the heart that thinks. For example, "As he thinks in his heart, so is he" (Prov. 23:7

NKJV). So for our purposes in this chapter, "heart" and "mind" will be used interchangeably. What we're really talking about is the core of who you are—what determines your thoughts, feelings, and ultimately actions.

"We see things not as they are, but as we are ourselves," says H. M. Tomlinson.[2] Yes, there are certain indisputable facts about our existence. Our age. The color of our hair. Our address. But much of our lives is open to interpretation. I'm not talking about relativity, in which we each get to choose our own version of truth. What I mean is simply this: ultimately we are spiritual beings, and that means much of our existence can't be measured or scientifically verified. We do most of our true living within the heart.

As a counselor and life coach, I've seen this acted out in two ways. In the first, I've watched women go through exceedingly difficult circumstances and come through them with joy, faith, and resilience. What they were experiencing was not their ultimate reality. On the other hand, I've watched many more women (including myself) turn even everyday struggles into insurmountable obstacles because of what they tell themselves about them.

Ladies, here's an uncomfortable statement: we are pretty good at making things worse than they have to be. Who wants to smack me? I do. I wish that weren't true. I'd love to give a big black marker to each of you one day and say, "Cross out that line. I totally missed it on that one." But over and over again, I've seen that what ultimately takes women down is not their circumstances but instead their responses to them.

While that may be uncomfortable to hear, it also leads to a lot of hope. Because it means that we can learn to face what life throws at us in a different way. We can learn to be resilient, have peace, and press forward even in challenging times. Doesn't that sound good? (Chocolate ice cream sounds good too. That also helps in hard times.)

Most of us know this is true at some level. We look at our wild thoughts and crazyville reactions and think, "Why in the world am I doing this?" But we simply don't know what else to do. That's what this chapter is all about. I want to equip you with specific solutions and strategies for those moments so you can respond differently. I want to make it possible for your "eyes to be full of light" so you can see your circumstances and situation in new ways.

## Your Beautiful Brain

Your brain is a masterpiece. An endless symphony of wonder happens between your ears every single day. Every thought, perception, and reaction is a result of a complex and intricately built system.

I believe understanding how the physical and spiritual intersect is important. It shouldn't surprise us to learn that our spirituality is wired into our very DNA and brain pathways. God is always making the spiritual tangible—creating the world, sending Jesus as "the Word made flesh" (see John 1:14), working in mysterious ways in the physical parts of you.

So let's talk about your brain. There are three primary parts.

### The Brain Stem

The brain stem is the most primitive and basic part of your brain. It sits at the base of your skull and has two responsibilities: survival and threat assessment. You've probably heard of the fight-or-flight response. That originates right here in this little place. If the brain stem senses danger, it immediately sounds the alarm, and your body responds either by getting ready to rumble or getting ready to run away. Here's the thing: the brain stem can't tell the difference between types of threats. So in our modern world, it treats the snarky remark your co-worker made the same way it would a bear charging out of the woods. Also, the brain stem doesn't like change. It's a status quo junkie. So any kind of change sets off the alarm bells—including when you decide to think differently.

## The Limbic System

If we had only the brain stem, we'd spend all of our time sleeping, fighting, eating, procreating, and running away. Picture the life of a lizard. The brain stem is about all they've got, and that pretty much sums up their existence. Thankfully, God decided to give us much, much more. After the brain stem does the basics, the limbic system gets a shot at responding to our circumstances. It has two primary roles that involve *emotion* and *connection*. The limbic system tells mothers to care for their young, helps couples bond, and matches up actual emotional responses to the initial impressions from the brain stem. It acts as a processor that interprets what's happening to us and assigns emotions to events. It also prioritizes what we should focus on. When it's done so, it sends the primary emotion to the final segment of the brain, the neocortex.

## The Neocortex

Up until now, we've had a response, but not a lot of logic has been involved. We have a perception from the brain stem and a corresponding emotion from the limbic system. Now all of that goes to the neocortex for analysis. This is when we begin to really think in words about what we're experiencing. The neocortex sits just behind your eyebrows, and it's ultimately the boss of the other two sections. It's where you make decisions, think deep thoughts, and ultimately determine a course of action. It's also the place where being "transformed by the renewing of your mind" (Rom. 12:2) actually happens.

In particular, the limbic system is like a little kid who needs reassurance from the parent who better understands the world. Imagine a child coming to a parent full of emotions too big to grasp. If mama scoops up the child, holds her close, and tells her there really are no monsters under the bed, then she begins to calm down and think differently about those shadows. However, if the parent were to respond, "Oh, no! That's terrible. We're doomed," then the child's response would be quite different.

This makes sense to us, and yet we often give the "we're doomed" message to our limbic system through our negative thoughts. Then, as any child would, the limbic system ratchets up the emotional level even more until we feel intensely negative emotions. This then also makes the brain stem more likely to sound the fight-or-flight response because it's increasingly sensitive to threats.

On and on the cycle goes: perceived threat, emotional reaction, corresponding thoughts, more emotion, more threats perceived.

## Transforming Your Mind

God knows this is the way our brains work. After all, he made them. And when we think in ways that correspond to his kingdom, this complex system is beautiful and life-giving. For example, we can face incredible obstacles that arouse emotions in us, but through truth and transforming our minds we can handle these tough situations with grace, peace, and even joy.

I share this because we tend to think of our minds as being on autopilot. We believe our emotions or patterns of thinking can't be changed because when we try to do so we feel a lot of resistance (remember, the brain stem is a status quo lover). That resistance makes us think what we're trying to do must be wrong, so we feel guilty and give up.

But our brains are actually amazingly flexible. We can learn to think in new ways, and when we do, we respond in new ways too. In *Wired for Joy*, author Laurel Mellin says:

> Over the last 20 years, research has shown that the source of most of our stress is the brain itself. Given the onslaught of stress in daily life, it can easily become wired to favor stress—to amplify the real stress in our lives and manufacture a sense of imminent danger, even when there is none. Each time the stress of the day overwhelms your capacity to effectively process it, there is a price to pay.[3]

While I don't agree with all of Mellin's perspectives in her book, when I read her insights into our brains, I can't help but see God's fingerprints all over the way we're made. Mellin goes on to share that our brains have two main types of circuitry: stress and joy. Stress comes more naturally to us, and it takes intentional change and obedience to the Spirit to learn to live in joy. But it is possible. In essence:

> It turns out that the emotion that feels the best—joy— is also best for our health. . . . Joy is the signpost that we are in a state of optimal coordination and smooth running of the operations of life. Wear and tear is at a minimum, aging slows, and, in every possible way, people are at their best.[4]

When Scripture says, "the joy of the LORD is your strength" (Neh. 8:10), it's speaking not just spiritual but physical, tangible truth. Isn't that amazing?

This explains why when someone says, "I'm fine," and they're actually not, we often don't really believe them. We can inherently sense when someone is saying one thing with the logical part of their brain but the other more emotional parts are not convinced. That leads us to ask things like, "How are you, *really*?" Our brain wiring is also the reason why clichés and Scripture verses slapped on a situation like a Band-Aid don't work for us either. They only address the logical parts of our minds while leaving the others out.

## Switching Tracks

The other day I pulled up to a railroad crossing just as a train came barreling through it. At the last minute, it screeched to a halt and an engineer jumped out of the first car. He ran to the track, made some adjustments, and hopped back in to continue the journey. As I looked closer, I could see exactly what he'd done—switched the track.

Our thoughts are a lot like that train. They go speeding through life, and we don't give much intentional focus to them. They run on automatic based on past experiences and how we've taught ourselves to respond to different situations. Every time you react a certain way, your brain makes a note of it. That means the thoughts you think most have the strongest tracks, and your mind automatically goes there. When you decide to "renew your mind," it means stepping off the train and switching the tracks. We have to do this again and again. Then at some point, your brain realizes that this is the new normal response, and it goes there automatically.

Psychology describes the four stages of change we go through in this way:

- *Unconscious incompetence*—We don't even realize the incorrect response we're having. For example, we don't know that chocolate doughnuts have 5,000 calories.

............
54

- *Conscious incompetence*—We know we need to change, but we don't know how. We read the doughnut box and realize we're in trouble but don't know what else to eat for breakfast.
- *Conscious competence*—We know how to change, but doing so requires intentional action on our part. We want to reach for the doughnut box but force ourselves to go for the whole grain muffin instead (it's a yummy one, not the cardboard kind).
- *Unconscious competence*—Our new responses and behaviors become automatic. We wake up craving whole grain muffins because our body has become so much healthier, and we don't even think about the doughnut.

When we think in terms of biblical change, the same process holds true as well. At first we don't even realize that we're sinners. Then we become aware of how we fall short, but we're not sure how to fix ourselves. We find out about Jesus and ask him to take over our lives. With his help our behavior begins to change. Over time, who we are and how we live are fully transformed.

In our microwave-instant-right-now society, we tend to think that change should happen as soon as we decide it's time. But it simply doesn't work that way. That's the neocortex talking, and it's the starting place for us to be different. But instant change, with very rare exceptions, simply isn't possible.

In her book *Unglued*, bestselling author Lysa TerKeurst describes this as "imperfect progress." She says:

> What kept me from making changes was the feeling that I wouldn't do it perfectly. I knew I'd still mess up and the changes wouldn't come instantly. Sometimes we girls think if we don't make instant progress, then real change isn't coming. But that's not so. There is a beautiful reality called *imperfect progress*. The day I realized the glorious hope of this kind of imperfect

change is the day I gave myself permission to believe
I really could be different.[5]

Lysa is describing the first step to real change: permission. As
long as we demand perfection from ourselves, then, ironically, we
will make little progress. When we lift those demands, then God
can move us forward.

The next step of true change is being intentional. In our society,
we tend to think that the primary part of change is *intellectual
commitment*. We tell ourselves, "I will do this from now on" or "I
will never do that again," and then we're surprised that we can't
follow through the way we'd like. But as I described above, intellectual commitment (the neocortex) is only the beginning point.
The rest of our minds must be transformed too. That means not
just intellectually committing our wills but also intentionally
taking action to change our response patterns. Doing so requires
two kinds of strategies: short-term and long-term.

Short-term strategies help us in the moment. Long-term strategies eventually turn into a lifestyle. Now let's talk about how that
happens in your beautiful brain.

## Strategies for Your Life

Amy tucks her kids into bed and one of them suddenly declares,
"Mom, I forgot my science project is due tomorrow!"

Sarah steps into a meeting at work and the first words spoken
are, "We're having layoffs."

Christy stares across the table into the eyes of her boyfriend
as he says, "Maybe we should see other people."

Miranda sits on the edge of her seat in the clinic as her doctor
shares the report with a sigh. "I'm sorry, but the cancer is back."

We will all face moments like these in different ways. What they have in common is their ability to go straight to the brain. Did you feel yourself tense up as you read them? Did an emotion like anxiety or dread begin to well up inside? Did you wonder, "What if that happened to me?" Then you've just experienced all three parts of your brain working together.

The important aspect is what comes next. What does Amy do after that declaration? Sarah when her career takes a sudden turn? Christy after she realizes her boyfriend may be breaking up with her? Miranda after she realizes she's going into battle again?

First, all four are going to have a *reaction*. They'll have a visceral response in which their pulse speeds up, their focus becomes more intense, and their body goes on hyper alert. Second, they are going to be flooded with emotion. Then an automatic thought is going to pop into their mind.

*A reaction is not optional.* It's the God-given way our bodies are wired, and we can't bypass it because to do so would be detrimental to our well-being. But we do get to choose what we do next.

## Short-Term Strategies

After the initial reaction comes, then we have the possibility of turning it into a *response*. Reactions are automatic, but responses are intentional. So what does that involve?

Here's where the strategies begin, and Romans 12:12 gives us a starting place: "Be joyful in hope, patient in affliction, faithful in prayer."

### ～ Be Joyful in Hope ～

A reaction always involves some kind of dashed hopes. In other words, interrupted expectations. We want to make it to work on time and there is a traffic jam. We want to get pregnant and the test is negative again. We want our spouse to quit drinking and we come home to find another six-pack gone. We hope, hope, hope, and then face disappointment. This sends our brain patterns into a tailspin. Yes, we will feel grief and frustration when this happens. That's totally normal, and it's okay. The option we do have is whether or not we'll let this take us into a downward spiral.

Mellin says that we have two primary types of circuits in our minds: stress circuits and joy circuits. The goal is to make the joy circuits the strongest, the ones we go to most often.

When you encounter a moment like the ones above, do the same thing you would if you suddenly caught on fire (because that's essentially what it's like in your brain): stop, drop, roll.

*Stop*—Before you take another step or speak a single word, take one deep breath. As you breathe in, notice what your body is doing. Is your heart beating fast? Are your palms sweaty? Do you feel tears coming to your eyes or are your fists clenching in anger? That's the brain stem preparing for fight or flight.

As you breathe out, notice the strongest emotion you're feeling. Are you hurt? Sad? Mad?

Here's why this matters: The brain stem and limbic system are communicators. And like any good messenger, if they don't feel heard, then they will repeat the message louder and with more intensity until it gets through. So if you ignore what they're telling you, it only gets worse. Occasionally, you may even experience an amygdala hijack—which means the brain stem temporarily overtakes the neocortex and all hope for logical thought in the moment is lost. Not fun for anyone.

*Drop*—After you take that deep breath in and out, identify the expectation that has just been shattered. Say, "I really wanted _____ , and that is not going to happen right now." Essentially, you are dropping the expectation you had just a few minutes before. In place of that expectation, you need to put words to reality. At this point, try to use objective words instead of emotional ones. "This is what's happening right now instead: _____."

*Roll*—Now that you've synced all three parts of the brain God has given you, it's time to determine a next step. How are you going to roll with this? One thing is for sure; you are not going to fix this problem right here and now. Thinking of how to do so will only overwhelm you and send the brain stem back into overdrive again. Pause and tell God what you've learned and seen. "God, I'm feeling really _____, I don't like that _____, is happening right now. Please help me and show me what to do. The next small step I'm going to take in this moment is _____."

Then take action. For example, the next step for the woman hearing about her cancer might be asking questions of the doctor (and she needs a clear mind to do so).

The point is to keep the train of your thoughts from suddenly starting to go a hundred miles an hour down the stress track. And that leads right into what comes next.

~ *Be Patient in Affliction* ~

The brain stem lives only in the present. It doesn't focus on the past. It doesn't have visions of the future. It is designed to keep you alive right here, right now. That means when it's triggered, it will holler like a two-year-old, "Make it better NOW, NOW, NOW!" So we polish off a gallon of ice cream, drain the extra glass of wine, or yell at our spouse. Then we wonder what in the world we were thinking. But that's exactly it—we weren't thinking at all.

We need patience in affliction because our initial reaction will almost always lead us astray. We have to intentionally resist the urge to do whatever our brain is demanding of us. Your brain, like that two-year-old, just doesn't know any better in that moment. It's scared or angry or in pain, and all it wants is for everything to be fixed.

But as the rest of your mind knows, life doesn't work that way. Tough situations don't usually resolve themselves in a matter of seconds. And more than any other, this is the time when it's easy to make choices that actually make things worse for us. So what do we do instead?

After your initial stop, drop, and roll response, find some quiet space to reflect as soon as you can. Go to the bathroom, take a walk, set up a coffee date with a trusted friend. Give yourself mental space to process what has happened. Only you know how you do that best. Here are some common types of processors:

- *Verbal*—If you are a verbal processor, you need to say your thoughts out loud before they make sense to you. If this is your style, find someone trustworthy to talk through the situation with you.

- *Internal*—If you are an internal processor, you need time by yourself to make sense of things. Give yourself permission to step outside your busy schedule and carve out time for pondering and praying.

- *Written*—If you are a written processor (I almost wrote "word processor," but that sounded funny), you're a hybrid of the above. You need to get your thoughts outside yourself, but you prefer to do so privately at first. Grab your laptop or a journal and let the words come.

- *Eventual*—If you are an eventual processor, there's often a time lapse between the event and when you feel the full emotional impact. If that's the case, you just need to note that at some point soon you're going to need to process in one of the ways above and prepare for it.

............

○ *Hands-on*—If you are a hands-on processor, simply thinking or reflecting is not enough for you. To clear your mind you need to physically do something like taking a bike ride, cleaning the house, or cooking a meal. Learn what works best for you.

One of my graduate school professors, Gary Oliver, likes to say, "If you bury an emotion, you bury it alive."[6] When we avoid what's happening, we eventually face it in another way. Being patient in affliction means not only persevering but also devoting the time needed to really deal with what's happening to us with the help of God and those who love us.

~ *Be Faithful in Prayer* ~

More than anything else it is God's help that makes the difference in difficult situations. Being faithful in prayer means inviting God into our circumstances. When our biological alarms go off, it's all too easy to say, "I'll just deal with this." Instead, when we stop, drop, and roll and then subsequently reflect, we can say, "God, help me. Be in this with me. Show me what to do."

In the Old Testament, the Israelite army was preparing to go into battle against what seemed like insurmountable odds. The commander utters a prayer that I love: "We do not know what to do, but our eyes are on you" (2 Chron. 20:12).

We don't have to know the answers. We don't have to have things figured out. All we really need to know is where to focus.

Prayer can be an intimidating venture. But throughout Scripture we see prayers of every length and kind.

○ *Short prayers*—Sentences like the one above can be uttered in a time of need.
○ *Long prayers*—Jesus spent forty days in the wilderness in prayer at one point in his ministry (see Matt. 4).

- ° *Written prayers*—Putting our prayers on paper can help us concentrate.
- ° *Communal prayers*—Believers often prayed for and with each other in times of trouble.
- ° *Creative prayers*—God made us in his image, and he is endlessly creative. Don't be afraid of trying a new way of talking to him.

Inviting God into our situations isn't a one-time event. It happens over and over again. And it's not just about speaking our needs to him; it's about listening too. We need to hear from him what he wants our response to be in a given situation. That's what replaces our natural reactions. It takes time to discern his voice above our emotions and physical reactions. But he is there and promises to guide us through his Spirit. The point of being transformed in our minds is that "then you will be able to test and approve what God's will is—his good, pleasing, and perfect will" (Rom. 12:2).

The words used there are "test and approve" not "instantly know" and "always do." What we're talking about here is a change in direction, not an immediate arrival at the destination. Switching the track of the train doesn't get it to the next station right away. It simply means we are on a new course.

Every time we do switch the track using the tools above as well as others, our minds become more likely to do so automatically the next time. To encourage that process, we can also implement long-term strategies that lead to a change in lifestyle.

## Long-Term Strategies

Until the middle of the twentieth century, most trains ran on steam. That meant coal or wood was burned, which created steam in a boiler that powered the train. In other words, what the train consumed became what drove it forward.

It's much the same with our minds. While our responses keep us on the right track, our overall thought patterns fuel the work of God in our lives. Without right thoughts, we get weighed down and stuck.

Perhaps the most well-known Scripture passage on our thoughts is from the apostle Paul:

> Finally, brothers and sisters, whatever is true, whatever is noble, whatever is right, whatever is pure, whatever is lovely, whatever is admirable—if anything is excellent or praiseworthy—think about such things. (Phil. 4:8)

I'd read these verses many times but hadn't really pondered what they meant. When I did so, I found many "lumps of coal" hidden within them that could fuel my thoughts in new ways.

~ *The Whatevers* ~

*Whatever is true*—The first thing to ask ourselves is, "Is this thought true?" Here's the thing: whatever we're thinking *feels* true. It's our internal reality. But that doesn't mean it *actually is* true. Test the thought against Scripture, and if you need to, ask a trusted friend for clarity.

"I feel lonely today" is true, while "Everyone hates me" is not.

*Whatever is noble, whatever is right*—Next we question, "If this is true, is it noble and right?" Noble and right both have meanings associated with moral character. Just because something is factually true doesn't mean it's worthy of our mental attention. In other words, is this thought pleasing to God?

"God did a good job on that handsome man" is noble, while "I wonder what it would be like to sleep with him" is not.

*Whatever is pure*—Even when a thought seems noble, we can ask, "Has anything slipped in to contaminate this thought?" In a world of half-truths and postmodernism, we need to be especially careful. When the enemy tempted Jesus in the wilderness, he didn't use outright lies—he used Scripture out of context. There was some truth but not *pure* truth.

"Sue's cake turned out well and sometimes that makes me jealous" is pure, while "Sue's cake turned out well because she's such a show-off, and I hope her icing melts" is not.

*Whatever is lovely, whatever is admirable*—We can ask, "What can I find in my day that is lovely and admirable?" This is about cultivating a habit of looking for the good in life. As we talked about before, none of us is wired this way naturally. Sure, some of us have sunnier dispositions than others. But because of how we're wired to survive, we all struggle with negativity. Being negative doesn't equal being "real." It's not easier or more authentic to find the negative. It's actually more courageous and challenging to look for the joy in a broken world. And here's the benefit: the more you look for it, the more of it you'll actually see.

"My friendship with Tara isn't perfect, but I love her strength, encouraging heart, and ability to see the best in everyone" is lovely and admirable. "I wish Tara would just get over herself and stop acting so fake all the time—she can't possibly be that happy" is not.

*Whatever is excellent or praiseworthy*—We can ask, "How can I see God's hand in my situation today?" This takes it one step beyond lovely and admirable. This is committing to seeing the divine intersect with our everyday existence and praising God for it even in the tough times. Perhaps this is last on the list because it's the toughest. It takes a lot of practice, and you will almost always feel like you are faking it at first. Remember that's not true—it simply feels that way because your brain loves the status quo and resists change. It takes time for it to adapt to new thought patterns in a way that feels natural.

"God, I really wish it hadn't rained today when we planned a picnic with the kids, but thank you for keeping us safe and giving us a few hours of sunshine" is excellent and praiseworthy. "This day is terrible and everything is ruined—why does this always happen to me?" is not.

It's much easier to just say "whatever" than to practice the "whatevers" above. But when we choose to practice them, over time our thoughts and lives change for the better.

### ∼ The Fruit ∼

Ultimately, we want our thoughts to be controlled by the Spirit and not our flesh. And we know that "the fruit of the Spirit is love, joy, peace, patience, kindness, goodness, faithfulness, gentleness, self-control" (Gal. 5:22–23 ESV).

So here's one more way to test your thoughts:

### — Thoughts Quiz —

Does this thought bring . . . ? (check the circle next to one)

| | |
|---|---|
| ○ Love | ○ Isolation |
| ○ Joy | ○ Depression |
| ○ Peace | ○ Anxiety |
| ○ Patience | ○ Striving |
| ○ Kindness | ○ Condemnation |
| ○ Goodness | ○ Shame |
| ○ Faithfulness | ○ Doubt |
| ○ Gentleness | ○ Harshness |
| ○ Self-control | ○ Self-punishment or Self-indulgence |

If all of the checks are on the right, the thought is not from God.

If some of the checks are on the right, there may be some truth, but there are lies too.

If all of the checks are on the left and the thought aligns with Scripture, it's of God.

## Replacing Your Thoughts

Once you've identified that a thought is untrue, then there's still another step. At that point, it's tempting to begin berating ourselves for what we're thinking, but that's not helpful. And as we talked about earlier, we're all making imperfect progress. Instead, use the questions above to help you discover God's perspective.

For example: "Everyone hates me."

Is this true? No.

Then what is true?

"I recently moved to this area, and I feel lonely right now. It takes time to build friendships. I need to remember that this isn't about me but about my circumstances. *God, you want me to be in community with others. Please bring me friends and show me how to reach out to others as well.*"

Does this mean the emotion of being lonely instantly goes away? Nope. But it will prevent the downward spiral that telling ourselves "everyone hates me" inevitably leads to, which only makes things worse.

*Now it's time for you to give it a try. Write down a thought that has been going through your mind lately:*

_____

_____

Now ask the questions above about it. Is it a thought that's true, noble, right, pure, lovely, admirable, excellent, or praiseworthy? Is it a thought filled with love, joy, peace, patience, kindness, goodness, faithfulness, gentleness, and self-control?

If the answer is yes, keep on thinking it!

*If the answer is no or not completely, then what can you replace it with instead? What is God's version?*

_____

_____

At this point, you might be feeling a little guilty about some of the thoughts running through your mind. But we are human and we all struggle with our thoughts. That's why "we take captive every thought to make it obedient to Christ" (2 Cor. 10:5). I love the word *captive* because it shows that God understands how our thoughts can be like wild little things that don't do what we'd like at all. We also *make* our thoughts obedient—they don't do so willingly. One by one we've got to take control of them, and that takes time, effort, and a lot of practice.

## The Joy Ahead

The good news? The outcome of going through the process above is that you begin to live in joy more and more—even in challenging times. Like we talked about, using the tools above will at first feel like a lot of work. But at some point when you least expect it, you will truly learn new ways of thinking, and they will become automatic. The process is similar to learning to ride a bike. It takes effort and a few bumps along the way, but eventually you've got it. And once you do, you never lose that skill.

Laurel Mellin describes getting to the point of consistently living in joy this way:

> Your physiology is balanced and your internal work-
> ings are at their best. You are present, balanced, and
> have positive emotions fueled by a sense of meaning

in your life. When in joy, the stress response is quiet, the relaxation response is activated, and surges of feel-good chemicals course through the reward pathways in the brain.[7]

The wonderful thing about getting to this place is that it transforms you into someone who can help others think and live this way too. You approach conflict differently. You talk about your day differently. You do family life differently. The world needs joyful people, especially now.

My grandmother has a sign hanging on her wall with a quote from Léon Bloy that says, "Joy is the most infallible sign of the presence of God." When we learn how to live with true joy, we display God in a way that's rare in our world.

It's not easy. It's not instant. But it is possible.

Your mind is a powerful, beautiful gift.

Use it well and wisely, friend.

# Your **Heart** Is Worth Guarding

She sends me a text and I can almost hear the sigh in her voice at the end of her words. "I said something I shouldn't have," she confesses. She goes on to share that she's especially frustrated with herself because she'd just been studying how we're to use our words for gratitude and praise.

Isn't that how it goes? We have good intentions, we know what's right, and then we go out and do the opposite.

Or maybe that's just my friend and me.

So many days I set out to do one thing and end up doing another. I struggle, repent, try again. This is *especially* true in times of stress.

My friend above shared the same. She's been under major pressure, and it finally came out of her mouth. I'm sure it felt good in the moment but left her feeling disappointed with herself and full of regret.

Why does that happen?

It's because *in times of stress our defenses are down.* We each have a threshold for what we can take before it becomes really tempting to do something we know we shouldn't. Stress takes us across that threshold much more quickly.

A popular method called HALT describes how this works. In essence, when we are Hungry, Angry, Lonely, or Tired, then we're more likely to make poor choices. This has been applied in areas as varied as from addiction recovery to parenting. What remembering HALT serves to do is to help us pause and recognize that we're vulnerable in some way. We need help of some kind. It might be rest, a good meal, or a conversation with a trusted friend.

HALT is just one tactic for dealing with these moments in our lives. There are many other strategies too. One verse in Proverbs sums them all up: "Above all else, guard your heart, for everything you do flows from it" (4:23).

When we say what we shouldn't, do what we swore we wouldn't, mess up in more ways than we knew we could, it doesn't begin right at that moment. Those are only outward displays of what's already brewing in our hearts. "The mouth speaks what the heart is full of" (Luke 6:45).

So when I say that our defenses are down in times of stress, what I really mean is that our hearts are unguarded. This happens to all of us. It's part of being human. The good news is that we can learn how to really guard our hearts.

Your heart is a treasure. As the verse above says, everything in your life flows from it. It's a wonderful, mysterious gift that God has given you. It holds so much of who you are and what he's called you to do. It's worth protecting.

............

## Signs of a Guarded Heart

What does a guarded heart look like? Let's picture a place that holds great value. In biblical times, that would have been a palace. Solomon, who wrote the book of Proverbs, was a king with great wealth. He had guards surrounding where he lived to protect all that was within. Those guards had several roles.

First, they would act as defenders and keep out anything or anyone that had evil intent. Second, they would let in what was needed—such as supplies or important guests. If anything did come within the palace that should not be there, those guards would have the duty of making sure it was sent back out. They would also let Solomon and others go out into the kingdom through the gates as needed.

Guarding our hearts works much the same way. It's not a static state but instead an in-and-out flow we carefully watch. Sometimes through life circumstances we end up focusing too much on one of these aspects. When that happens, our hearts can fall into one of these states:

- *Lockdown*—Our hearts are closed. Nothing can come in, and nothing can go out. We feel isolated and alone. Perhaps even hard and bitter. But the risk of opening up is simply too great.

- *Open wide*—Our hearts are unprotected. We let anything and anyone in, even if it's harmful. We may feel unvalued, of little worth, and so we don't feel as if this precious part of who we are deserves to have boundaries.

- *Exit only*—Our hearts aren't completely closed down. We feel comfortable giving to others and meeting their needs. But we are unable or unwilling to receive. The only direction is out, and we're often exhausted.

- *Entrance only*—Our hearts can receive, but we don't pass it on to others. We've somehow believed the lie that life is all about us. We take and take, then wonder why we still feel so empty all the time.

These descriptions are extremes, but we can all probably identify times we've been in each of these states at different points in our lives.

What keeps us from falling into these patterns is learning what it means to have a heart that's guarded instead. This matters all the time but is even more important when we face challenges or difficulties.

Imagine you're standing in Solomon's courtyard. All around you is the bustle of people coming and going. Activity is happening. Colors, food, and music abound. The air is filled with vitality and life. You smile as you are caught up in the flow of what's around you. More than anything else, the word *flow* describes what a guarded heart is supposed to feel like: "Everything you do flows from it" (Prov. 4:23). That happens in several ways when our hearts are truly guarded.

## When Your Heart Is Guarded, Emotions Are Felt and Expressed Appropriately

Sandra pushes back her hair and wipes the last traces of mascara from under her eyes. She opens the door to her car in the church parking lot, steps out, and squares her shoulders. "Sandra!" a voice calls out from a few feet away. "How are you?"

Sandra smiles so hard it hurts and answers, "Oh, I'm great! How are you?"

When Sandra locks away her emotions time after time, she shuts down her heart. It *feels* like her heart is guarded. After all, life seems so much safer this way. But that's not what guarding really means. Having a guarded heart means our emotions can be felt and expressed freely.

Of course, we need to use discernment in doing so. The greeter in the parking lot might not have been the right person to hear about Sandra's woes. But she needs *someone* who can listen and understand.

The first person we can go to is God. But unfortunately, myths about our emotions often keep us from processing with him. We label certain emotions "good" and others "bad," so we share only part of what we're feeling. But all emotions are neutral—even anger, which perhaps gets the worst rap of all. Yes, there are verses like "in your anger do not sin" (Eph. 4:26). That means we all experience anger—even Jesus did—and what matters is our response to it.

By understanding that emotions simply communicate to us what is happening in our lives, we can learn to listen to them, express them, and ask God what he wants us to do.

We also need someone to be "Jesus with skin on," as my friend Deidra Riggs likes to say. We are made for connection and community, for authenticity. A guarded heart helps us find safe people to confide in. We build relationships slowly over time, and when someone is trustworthy, we let them into our lives—the happy parts and hard parts too.

What Sandra doesn't know is that the person that greeted her in the church parking lot is having her own struggle too. Just minutes before, Cheri had been screaming at the top of her lungs at her children on the ride to church. A hurried morning with some small mistakes quickly turned into a reason for full-out venting. When Cheri pulled into the parking lot, she regained her senses. While releasing all that emotion felt good moments before, she now felt only shame and regret. She noticed Sandra getting out of her car. "Why can't I just be more calm like her?" she sighed to herself.

Cheri's heart is also unguarded, just in a different way. Instead of keeping everything in, she lets it all out. She's heard that "venting" is good for you, but she can't figure out quite how. Sure, it feels great at the time, but it seems to only add more hurt and distance in her relationships. When she's not shouting out loud, she's yelling at herself on the inside. She thinks if she just keeps trying to get all of her emotions out, then surely one day they'll be gone and she'll be at peace at last.

What Cheri is missing is self-control. We're never told to let our emotions have mastery over us. We're to respond to difficult situations with wisdom and kindness. Even research now verifies that "venting" does more harm than good. We are to "speak the truth in love" (Eph. 4:15), and a guarded heart enables us to do so. We can share how we're feeling without damaging others or ourselves.

If you find yourself having a moment like Sandra or Cheri (and we all do), it's not too late. You can pause and take these steps to begin guarding your heart again.

## Identify What You're Feeling

First, put what you feel into simple, objective words. Paul Ekman studied emotions all over the world. He found that across cultures, there are six basic feelings common to every human being. So if you're not sure how to describe your emotion, pick one of these six as a starting place: anger, disgust, fear, happiness, sadness, surprise.[1]

Here are some additional words for how you may feel:

## — *Common Emotions* —

- Afraid
- Amused
- Angry
- Annoyed
- Anxious
- Ashamed
- Blessed
- Bold
- Bored
- Brave
- Broken
- Calm
- Cautious
- Certain
- Cheerful
- Comfortable
- Cautious
- Certain
- Cheerful
- Comfortable
- Compassionate
- Competent
- Confident
- Confused
- Content
- Courageous
- Defensive
- Delighted
- Depressed

- Determined
- Disgusted
- Ecstatic
- Embarrassed
- Empty
- Encouraged
- Enraged
- Enthusiastic
- Envious
- Excited
- Exhausted
- Fearful
- Foolish
- Forgiven
- Free
- Frightened
- Frustrated
- Fulfilled
- Furious
- Giddy
- Glad
- Grateful
- Grieved
- Guilty
- Happy
- Hopeful
- Humble
- Hurt
- Hysterical

- Jealous
- Joyful
- Lazy
- Lonely
- Loved
- Mad
- Overwhelmed
- Peaceful
- Pressured
- Protected
- Quiet
- Sad
- Satisfied
- Scared
- Shocked
- Shy
- Silly
- Strong
- Supported
- Surprised
- Suspicious
- Sympathetic
- Timid
- Understood
- Valued
- Weary
- *Add Yours Here...*

It seems like a basic thing to do, but we often don't even know what we're feeling. When we put it into words, we move the emotion into the neocortex that we talked about in the last chapter—the seat of rational thinking.

## Figure Out the Trigger

After you've identified the emotion, ask God to show you the source. Why are you feeling this way? Write down the first thing that comes to mind. Then ask yourself if this is *really* it. We may think our kids are driving us nuts when it's actually that we're exhausted from staying up late last night to finish a report.

Important note: the "why" we're talking about is *the immediate why*, the most recent trigger—not the *analytical why* that explains something for all time. An immediate why is, "I skipped lunch and now I feel really irritable." It's not, "When I was a kid someone teased me about eating too much, which led me to hide cookies in my room, so I got grounded and . . ." An immediate why is not about the past. It's about right now. It's valid at times to analyze those deeper "why" questions. But I firmly believe that it's best not to do that on our own—and especially not when we're stressed. If a thought like that pops into your mind, write it down and talk it through at a later time with a trusted friend or counselor.

## Know What You Need

Once you know what you're feeling and the immediate why, it's time to figure out what you actually need. This is especially important for women because we are prone to "rumination." That's a fancy term for going over things again and again in our minds. It feels effective, but it actually only intensifies our original response—either locking down our hearts or having an emotional free-for-all. So it's vital to identify a need that we actually have right now. Some examples of needs are: sleep, food, companionship, help, or truth. (Note: Your mind will first suggest things like cookies, slapping someone, or running away to Hawaii. That's entirely normal. Just smile and keep going until you figure out what you *really* need.)

## Make a Plan

Once you know what you need, it's time to make a game plan. What steps are you going to take to meet that need? Generally, the smaller and more specific the better. It works best if you can at least do something to change the situation in a tiny way in the next five minutes. If that's not possible, write down a time when you can get that need met. For example, if you're exhausted, then commit to going to bed at 9:00 p.m. that night.

## Reclaim Truth

Finally, when our hearts are unguarded emotionally, the enemy will try to take advantage of the opportunity. You will probably hear some kind of lie that goes along with what you're feeling. So after you've worked through these steps, ask God to show you what truth you need to believe right now.

Your emotions might be saying, "You are unloved," but God says, "I have loved you with an everlasting love" (Jer. 31:3).

Your emotions might be telling you, "You have completely blown it," but God says, "I work all things together for good for those who love me" (see Rom. 8:28).

Your emotions might be insisting, "You have no hope" but God says, "I have a hope and future for you" (see Jer. 29:11).

· · · · · · · · · · · **Putting It All Together** · · · · · · · · · · ·

When you put all of the steps above together, it looks like this:

*A strong emotion hits you, so you go through this process:*
° I am feeling:

_____

_____

- Because (first thing that comes to mind):

  _____

  _____

- Is this really the reason?
  - If **yes**, then continue.
  - If **no**, then write a new reason below:

  _____

- What do I need right now?

  _____

  _____

- What's the first small thing I'm going to do about that need?

  _____

  _____

- What truth do I need to believe in this moment?

  _____

  _____

Sometimes we experience more than one emotion at a time. "Even in laughter the heart may ache" (Prov. 14:13). If that's true of you, work through this exercise as many times as you need to in order to identify all of them.

When you experience and express emotions the way God intended, you are guarding your heart. You're also guarding your relationships and your very life.

## When Your Heart Is Guarded, Relationships Are Based on Give and Take

Our emotions never happen in isolation. While we feel them internally, they are almost always tied to external circumstances and those around us.

Other people can bring us great joy or much frustration—and quite often both. Some of those frustrations can be avoided by looking at how God set up relationships to work. A search of the New Testament reveals the phrase "one another" many times. A guarded heart has "one another" relationships rather than the following alternatives:

- *One below the other*—In this type of relationship, you find that you are always serving someone else's needs. You may feel controlled, overlooked, or manipulated. If you try to assert yourself or share your needs, the response may be anger, a withdrawal of affection, or even threats. A woman in an abusive relationship is experiencing the "one below the other" dynamic.
- *One above the other*—When this form of relationship is in place, you are firmly in control. You practice authority over others and demand "my way or the highway." You may do so out of fear, but the ultimate result is that you feel alone. You may gain compliance from others but not true connection. A woman who manipulates her family into doing what she wants is displaying a "one above the other" scenario.

- *One is the other*—Sometimes we merge our identity with another person. Psychology calls this "enmeshment." It's hard to tell where we end and the other person begins. Rather than interdependence, there is great dependence. In some ways, the other person is an idol. A woman who falls so "madly in love" that she turns her back on her values and other relationships is in a "one is the other" situation.
- *One with no other*—If we practice any of the above for a period of time, we end up getting hurt, and so do those around us. At this point, we may decide it's time to turn into a "relational desperado." We go through life alone and value our ability to be completely independent. A woman who has been hurt by her best friend and decides she will never have friends again has decided "one with no other" is the relationship style she prefers.

The examples above are extremes, but we can probably find ourselves in each of them a little bit. Which one do you drift toward most? I occasionally get entangled in "one below the other" relationships. I find myself doing all the giving and then wonder why I begin to feel resentful. This isn't irreparable—it just means that I need to recognize it and change my behavior. When we get into unhealthy relationships, it's easy to blame the other person, but we need to take responsibility for our role as well. (Note: If you are in an abusive relationship, this is entirely different. In this case, you should seek professional guidance and physically remove yourself from the situation as quickly as possible.)

I'm not sure how it creeps into our thinking that we aren't really supposed to have "one another" relationships. I think as women we are especially vulnerable in this area. I remember sitting in a counselor's office a few years ago and asking, "Do you think God really wants us to have equal relationships?" The counselor looked at me as if I'd swallowed an alien. Her response made me begin to take a closer look to see if what I thought of as a healthy relationship and what Scripture promoted were actually the same thing.

So what does "one another" really mean? Much of the New Testament is instructing the early church how to get along with each other, how to not only love Jesus but also love each other. Through those letters we discover eleven important characteristics of "one another" relationships.

*Love* (John 13:34)—In our culture, the word *love* gets tossed around like a football. We say we love chocolate, television, and our spouses. Biblical love differs in that it's primarily about action—the way we treat each other. None of us is perfect, and we will all mess up at times. But overall, we are called to love each other well.

Ask: What's one way I'm loving others? How has someone loved me?

*Devotion* (Rom. 12:10)—Devotion is love that hangs in there over time. It means I'm consistently there for you and you're there for me. It means I don't give up on you when a more appealing option comes along. I'm committed for the ups and downs of our lives.

Ask: What's one way I've been there for someone else through his or her highs and lows? How has someone been there for me?

*Honor* (Rom. 12:10)—In the full context, this verse says we are to "honor one another above ourselves." This can lead some to believe "one below the other" relationships are actually what God wants. But I don't believe this is true. We are naturally selfish, so God is asking us to elevate others. The key is that *they are to do the same for us*. If this never happens, it's not a "one another" relationship. Honor is essentially respect: it means we act in ways that show we value each other's time, gifts, emotions, and other resources.

Ask: What's one way I honor others and consider their needs before my own? How has someone else honored me?

*Harmony* (Rom. 12:16)—I love the word *harmony* because it's a musical term about different parts blending together. We can sometimes interpret harmony as meaning we have to be like everyone else or stifle who God has made us to be. But that's not the case. Instead, we're to share life and appreciate what we have in common as well as the ways we're uniquely created.

Ask: What's one way I value the differences of others and appreciate how God has made them? How has someone showed me I'm valued for who I am even though we're different?

*Acceptance* (Rom. 15:7)—It's easy to judge each other. We complain, criticize, and condemn without even realizing the damage we're doing. Acceptance changes that and transforms our hearts into safe places where others can grow. Acceptance means I won't gossip about you, force you to be more like me, or look down on you. We accept each other because that is what Jesus did for us.

Ask: What's one way I am a safe person for others in my words, thoughts, and actions? How has someone else accepted me?

*Instruction* (Rom. 15:14)—In this context, Paul is telling the early Christians they are capable of teaching and helping each other grow. In our personality-driven culture, we can label some as "having all the answers." But that pushes those people into "one above another" dynamics. Yes, we have teachers and leaders who have been placed there by God. But we can all learn from each other in different ways, and doing so requires humility and openness.

Ask: What's one way I'm sharing my life with others as well as learning from their thoughts and experiences? Who is helping me learn and grow?

*Encouragement* (2 Cor. 13:11)—To encourage means "to fill with courage." We help each other be stronger, go farther, and do more than we thought we could. When we fall down, we help each other up. Encouragement lightens our load and helps us to finish the race God has given us well. While words are one form of encouragement, there are many other types, including the rest of the characteristics below.

Ask: What's one way I encourage others? How has someone encouraged me?

*Service* (Gal. 5:13)—Another characteristic that requires humility is service. It's easy to relate to others in a "what's in it for me?" way. This is actually the natural human response. Instead, Jesus asks us to set that aside and do what he did by serving. Again, it's not supposed to look like "I serve all the time and no one serves me." It's intended to be reciprocal service where everyone benefits and God is glorified.

Ask: What's one way I'm serving others? How has someone else served me?

*Kindness* (Eph. 4:32)—Kindness means we practice being sensitive to the needs of others. We're thoughtful and considerate. When they're hurting, we seek to comfort them. When they're rejoicing, we share the joy. We try to avoid being destructive to others with our words or what we do. We take the time to really understand the people in our lives.

Ask: What's one way I show kindness and compassion to others? How has someone demonstrated these qualities with me?

*Forgiveness* (Col. 3:13)—No matter how hard we try, we are going to mess up. So are the other people in our lives. It's simply part of being imperfect humans in a fallen world. We will hurt each other. We will let each other down. We will do the opposite of all the qualities above. That doesn't mean we need to cut ourselves off from community. It simply means that learning to love each other well is a lifelong process.

Ask: What's one way I've extended forgiveness to others? How has someone forgiven me?

*Hospitality* (1 Pet. 4:9)—This word is not about cake plates and pretty wreaths. Instead, true hospitality starts with the heart. It means we invite people into our lives. We enter into theirs as well. It can be as simple as a smile or as complex as weekend guests. What matters most is that we are communicating to others, "You have a place in my life and my heart."

Ask: What's one way I show hospitality to others? How has someone else made me feel welcome?

Which one of the characteristics above are you drawn to most? When you think of your relationships, how do these words fit with them?

While these words are to be true of our relationships, how they are acted out will look different with various people. Part of guarding our hearts is understanding that we simply *can't connect with everyone all the time*. Even Jesus didn't do so. He had the three closest disciples, then the twelve, then the forty, and finally the multitudes. He spent his time and emotional energy effectively. In other words, he guarded his heart.

Many of us feel guilty because we think we should be able to love everyone in the same way. But that's simply not what Jesus asks. Instead he invites us to a lifestyle of give-and-take relationships that are led by his Spirit. "One another" is the reality our hearts are made for, and they thrive most and love best when that's the way we relate to others.

## When Your Heart Is Guarded, Jesus Is on the Throne

Of course, the most important relationship of all is not one we have with another person. Instead, it's our connection to God himself. The only way we can truly love others is to experience his love first. For that to happen, we need to surrender our desire to run our own lives and hearts.

Author and pastor Pete Wilson says:

> We all long for more of something in our lives. We all treasure something or someone above our everyday experiences. We all give our devotion to somebody or something. These impulses are a part of our DNAs, etched into our natures, as normal and natural as breathing. I believe they have been placed inside our souls by our Creator God.
>
> Simply put, we are a people wired to worship. The question isn't, "Do we worship?" The question is, "Who (or what) do we worship?"[2]

The most unguarded heart of all is the one that does not know its master. We've all seen people like this. They fall head over heels in love and place their worth in one person. When that doesn't work out, they throw themselves into their careers. Then they get laid off. So they decide maybe it's time to move to a new place. They do so and end up getting married after all. So they start believing children will finally fill their emptiness. On and on they go, moving from one ruler of their hearts to the next, always ultimately being disappointed.

We all know people like this because we *are* all people like this. Or at least we have the capacity to be. On our own, we will always fall for lesser gods. We will serve anything and everything and most of all ourselves.

But we don't have to go through life this way. There's a different choice we can make. Jesus said, "Seek first his kingdom and his righteousness, and all these things will be given to you as well" (Matt. 6:33).

Can you hear what he is really offering here? He is saying, "Let me be on the throne of your life, and I will give you everything else your heart desires too." Oh, maybe not right away or in the way we expect. But the more we love him, the more our desires align with his, and we finally find the satisfaction we've been so desperately seeking in so many other places.

What makes this so hard? I believe it comes down to one simple word: control. Ever since Eden when the enemy told Eve she could be like God if she'd only eat the fruit, we've stretched out our hands to take control of our lives. We are content serving lesser gods because they don't seem as threatening. We tell ourselves we can manage the career, make the kids obey, ensure that person changes once we're married. But the God of the universe? Who knows what will happen if we turn our lives over to him. It takes a tremendous amount of trust.

But God isn't on a cosmic power trip. He's not asking for the throne of your life so he can boss you around and make you miserable. He's doing so first because he's God and he rightfully deserves that place. But also because he's the only one who can love you perfectly. *He's the only one who can truly guard your heart.* If you have children, why do you parent them rather than letting them do whatever they want? It's because you love them. It's much the same way with God. He wants to take care of our hearts, save us from ourselves, stop us from wasting our lives chasing after what he knows will ultimately only destroy us.

None of us lets God have the throne of our hearts all the time. But at any time we can stop and say, "God, I have tried to run my own life. I have chased after idols that can never satisfy. I realize that I am made to worship, and I want you to be on the throne of my life. Please take your rightful place. Please guard my heart and lead my life. Amen." We repeat that process over and over again. And we also invite Jesus into every moment of our lives.

There's only one other place that the phrase "guard your heart" appears other than in Proverbs: "Do not be anxious about any-thing, but in every situation, by prayer and petition, with thanksgiving, present your requests to God. And the peace of God, which transcends all understanding, will guard your hearts and your minds in Christ Jesus" (Phil. 4:6–7).

Do you see the beautiful offer God is making here? He is saying, "You can come to me with anything, anytime. Tell me what you need. I will give you peace that's greater than any circumstance. No matter what happens, I will protect your heart."

You have a King sitting on the throne of your heart who loves you more than you can even dare to dream. He will take care of you, and he will watch over the secret places of your heart with his love and grace.

## A Guarded Heart for Life

Learning to guard our hearts is a lifelong process. How will we know it's working?

- Our emotions will become more stable.
- Our relationships will be stronger.
- Our connection with Jesus will grow to deeper intimacy.
- Our ability to say yes as well as no will increase.
- Our lives will begin to be filled with more peace and less stress.
- Our focus will be on what's best and we'll be distracted less from God's purpose for us.
- Our joy will continue to expand.

Notice all of the words I used above are ongoing. Of course we want all those things right now. Who wouldn't? But as Proverbs

4:18 says, "The path of the righteous is like the morning sun, shining ever brighter till the full light of day." In other words, "We ain't in heaven yet." What we're looking for is a little more light each day, each week, each year.

It's not a light that we can see with our eyes but instead one that glows from deep down inside, from the deepest part of who we are. It comes from the One who sits on the throne in our hearts until we come before his throne in eternity. That's the day our hearts will be even more than guarded—they'll be fully free.

Forever and ever.

Amen.

# 5

# You Can Keep from
# **Sabotaging** Yourself

I'll never forget the first time I heard Whitney Houston sing. I was still in elementary school and just beginning to think about boys when her hit "I Want to Dance with Somebody" became one of the most frequently played tunes on my little radio. Houston never really stopped looking for someone to dance with her. She went from partner to partner—men, drugs, fame—and each left her feeling empty. She struggled with insecurity throughout her life until an early death connected to addiction silenced her. Diane Sawyer once asked Whitney, "If you had to name the devil . . . the biggest devil [in your life]?" Houston responded, "That would be me."[1]

We know we have a very real enemy of our souls, but sometimes it seems the biggest enemy we have to face is the one staring back at us in the mirror each morning. If I could sum up my work with women as a counselor and life coach, most often it would simply be this: helping them get out of their own way. The biggest struggle in my life is much the same: getting out of my own way.

This battle is age-old. Even the apostle Paul faced it:

> I do not understand what I do. For what I want to do I do not do, but what I hate I do. And if I do what I do not want to do, I agree that the law is good. As it is, it is no longer I myself who do it, but it is sin living in me. For I know that good itself does not dwell in me, that is, in my sinful nature. For I have the desire to do what is good, but I cannot carry it out. For I do not do the good I want to do, but the evil I do not want to do—this I keep on doing. Now if I do what I do not want to do, it is no longer I who do it, but it is sin living in me that does it.
>
> So I find this law at work: Although I want to do good, evil is right there with me. For in my inner being I delight in God's law; but I see another law at work in me, waging war against the law of my mind and making me a prisoner of the law of sin at work within me. What a wretched man I am! (Rom. 7:15–24)

Paul goes on to ask the question that our souls cry out as well: "Who will rescue me from this body that is subject to death?" (Rom. 7:24). We need a rescuer. We need someone to save us from ourselves. We need a power greater than our own. Paul knows who that is: "Thanks be to God, who delivers me through Jesus Christ our Lord!" (Rom. 7:25).

Because of Jesus, we don't have to sabotage ourselves. We can live differently. We can get out of our own way.

When we think of what trips people up, obvious things come to mind like addictions and infidelity. But as I've worked with women, I've discovered those are usually only symptoms. They are the ways we seek to soothe ourselves from the pain of self-sabotage. The real sources are often much deeper and more subtle.

# Why Do We Sabotage Ourselves?

She walks through the door of my counseling office. Sitting down, she shakes her head in dismay. "I totally blew it," she says. "I can't believe it. I was doing so well and then I completely messed up. What happened?" I nod with empathy—how many times have I done the same?

"It's actually normal to have a relapse after a lot of progress," I say. "It doesn't seem anyone ever gets it right the first time, or sometimes even the tenth!"

A hint of light begins to creep back into her eyes. "You mean this doesn't mean I'm a total failure?"

"Nope," I say. "It just means it's time to try again."

I go on to explain to her how our brains and bodies work. We are made for a fancy term called *homeostasis*. What that means is that we always seek ways to return to the status quo. That serves us well most of the time. For example, physically we sweat so our temperature stays steady. Socially we crave connection so we're able to maintain bonds over time with the same people. Emotionally we eventually even out after a tough day.

But there's one area in which homeostasis is not our friend quite as much: when we try to change. When we seek to alter a pattern in our lives, we *always* feel resistance. There's just no way around it. That's why we can intellectually commit to being different, but making it happen is much more complicated and messy.

Change takes a lot of emotional, spiritual, and physical energy. Here's another word for that: *stress*. And what do we do when we're stressed? We look for ways to ease the pain. That's what often leads us into addictions or immoral relationships. That doesn't make those choices okay, but it does explain why just when we are attempting to do what God wants, temptation rears its ugly head more than ever before.

I say this now because I want to talk through some of the common ways women sabotage themselves. As you read the following sections, I'm sure you'll agree that a lot of what I'm saying is true, but it will also feel hard to do, which can make us feel guilty. So I want to say up front: no guilt (we'll actually talk about that in a minute). Also, it's totally normal for all of this to be tricky to overcome. There is no super-duper Christian woman out there who does all these things. It doesn't come easy for any of us. But again, there is a difference between easy and possible.

We don't have to tackle these issues alone. As Paul said, it's Jesus who rescues us from this body of death. It is hard for us to change, but through his Spirit it can happen! Our goal for this chapter is not overnight transformation. Instead, it's first to recognize these battles in our lives for what they are, and then to take *one small step* to becoming our allies instead of our worst enemies.

Women tend to sabotage themselves in four main areas: emotional, social, spiritual, and physical—especially in the stressful times of life.

## Emotional Sabotage: Expectations

Whitney Houston had numerous voices speaking into her life: fans, media, the music industry, and friends and family who may not always have had her best interests in mind. No matter what she did, someone criticized her or told her she needed to be different or better in some way.

At some point, it seems she began to believe what she heard. It became her own voice that was telling her those things. That put her in an impossible place. No matter how much success she had, it could never be enough.

Can you relate? You clean the house but still think about your friend who mentioned that she vacuums every day. You finally manage to spend time reading the Bible only to remember your college roommate who could pray for an hour. You exercise and lose a few pounds only to flip open a magazine and see a woman who looks like she's never had a dessert in her life. And suddenly nothing you do will ever be enough.

So you feel depressed, become anxious, and eat a box of doughnuts that gets crumbs all over your clean floor. Yes, ma'am.

In *You're Already Amazing,* I talk about confronting the lie of expectations in my life. At one point, I found myself running ragged trying to complete an internal to-do list that would make even the Proverbs 31 woman faint with exhaustion. I finally told God I'd had enough. And it sorta seemed like he liked that idea. Then this thought drifted into my spirit: "Living under expectations is like living under the law. And Jesus has set me free to be a woman of grace."

Let that really sink in for a minute: *living under expectations is the modern version of living under the law.*

That became a turning point for me. I realized that I am a servant with one grace-giving master. I'm to love all, but I have to please only One. And that One is not me or anyone else in my life—he's the God who created me.

We tend to equate being loving with meeting expectations. For example:

○ "If I am a loving mom, then the house will always be clean."
○ "If I am a loving wife, then I will cook like Rachael Ray every night."
○ "If I am a loving friend, then I will be available anytime someone calls."

- ° "If I am a loving co-worker, then I will take on more than my share of the load."
- ° "If I am a loving church member, then I will volunteer for every committee."

But meeting the expectations of others and being loving are two entirely different things. We are never, anywhere in all of Scripture, told to meet the expectations of others.

The life of Jesus gives us a great example. He blew every expectation of what the Messiah would be like. He frustrated his disciples, confused his family, slipped away from the crowds. The way his life turned out didn't even come close to what people wanted. But it was exactly what God wanted. And because of that, it was what people really needed.

Taking on expectations will wear you out, exhaust you, and let you down. People are fickle. The moment you meet one standard, they'll change it or come up with another. Just take a look at fashion. That dress you maxed out the credit card on might have been great for one evening, but now this year's style is totally different and you're shopping again.

Here's a hard truth: people are not usually pleaseable. We're just not. None of us. We're fickle and selfish. We're moody and change our minds in a flash.

We can't live to meet each other's expectations. If we do so, we're destined for exhaustion and burnout. And we will find an outlet to soothe our hurts—whether that's too much alcohol, food, escaping into television, or something else.

To be women who live freely, we have to release ourselves and each other from expectations. They are prison bars God never intended for us.

In place of expectations, Jesus gives us *invitations*. He tells us, "Come to me, all you who are weary and burdened, and I will give you rest" (Matt. 11:28). And what burdens us more than expectations?

God whispers to our hearts, "I know you can't ever live up to my standards. That's why I sent Jesus. You are free from striving. You can live in grace, and I will help you grow. I accept you as you are, and I will be with you as you joyfully become all I've created you to be."

So how do you know if something is an expectation or an invitation?

| Expectations | Invitations |
| --- | --- |
| ◦ Are absolute ("You must...") | ◦ Are an extension of grace ("Come to me...") |
| ◦ Include punishment, either actual or implied ("Or else...") | ◦ Include forgiveness ("If you mess up, try again...") |
| ◦ Discourage us | ◦ Encourage us |
| ◦ Push us down, hold us back | ◦ Lift us up, move us forward |
| ◦ Require perfection | ◦ Offer growth |
| ◦ Cause us to strive | ◦ Free us to love |
| ◦ Lead us into temptation because we're seeking relief | ◦ Help guard us against temptation because we're thriving |
| ◦ Make us feel condemned | ◦ Teach us our true worth |
| ◦ Are about judgment | ◦ Are about acceptance |
| ◦ Start with humans | ◦ Start with God's heart |

When you feel a weight that's heavy on your shoulders, pause and ask, "Is this an expectation?" What's truly from God is not intended to weigh us down.

We sabotage ourselves when we take on expectations because they're simply too much for us to carry. God invites us to trade those demands for the lightness of grace and real love instead.

*What's one expectation you've been trying to fulfill? What's the invitation God wants to replace it with instead? (For example: I feel I must be perfect, but God asks me only to be growing.)*

---

---

---

## Social Sabotage: Giving In to Our Signature Insecurities

In reading about Whitney Houston's life, it became clear the criticisms that stung her most were those related to her greatest gifts. The same is true of all of us. While we may struggle with a variety of insecurities ranging from our hair to our ability to make small talk, we usually have one or two signature insecurities that give us the most angst. I've found in connecting with thousands of women that those insecurities are always tied to our gifts and God's calling on our lives.

For example, this is my signature insecurity: I fear that my heart will be misunderstood and that I will hurt my relationships. In almost every situation in which I find myself facing tons of fear or acting irrationally, it comes back to this insecurity. The reason? One of the gifts God has given me is connecting with the hearts of women and encouraging them.

A few years ago I made a career transition. I knew it was what God wanted me to do, but I was terrified. In spite of my company being wonderful in the process and my co-workers extending grace, I found myself locked in a cycle of anxiety and worry. My life coach, Denise Martin, finally called me on it (I love it when she does that). She asked me insightful questions until we both realized it wasn't the career changes scaring me. Instead, I was worried about how the transition would make people perceive my motives as well as what it could do to my deeply valued relationships with co-workers.

She had me list each person I thought might be impacted by this decision. Then she suggested I make an action plan for addressing each one individually to make sure the relationship remained strong. As I made the list, a shocking thing happened. I realized that *about half of the people on the list didn't even work at the company anymore.* In my mind and heart, they were still associated with it and with me, but it turned out most of my fears didn't have any basis in reality! As for the remainder of the list, I did talk to each one, and our relationships made the transition just fine.

A friend of mine has a gift for building community, so she has a signature insecurity of fearing that she will be left out. Another has a gift for being able to bring peace and stability to the lives of others, so she has a signature insecurity of fearing change. A woman at church I know has a gift for bringing comfort, so her signature insecurity is fearing she will hurt the feelings of others, which can cause her to hold back what she has to offer.

Your signature insecurities are always related to the ways God uses you most. Think of the last time you felt insecure.

*What was the situation you were in when you felt insecure?*

_____

_____

*What were you afraid would happen?*

_____

_____

*Why would it matter to you if that did happen?*

_____

_____

The answer to the third question probably gives you a glimpse into a core part of who you are, what you value, and how God uses you. *We are most vulnerable to insecurity in those places.*

*Based on the answers to the questions above, what do you think your signature insecurity might be?*

_____

_____

If you're not sure, that's totally normal. Figuring it out often requires the perspective of someone else (like Denise with me) or simply intentionally observing your reactions over time. If nothing came to mind, simply leave the space above blank and ask God to reveal anything you need to see in the coming days or weeks.

Once you know (at least vaguely) what your signature insecurity is, then it's time to make a plan for how to deal with it. Here's the thing: your signature insecurity is not going away completely. That's because it's tied too much to your strengths and gifts. For it to change, a lot of the important parts of who you are would need to as well.

What can be different is how you respond when you feel insecure. This is the point where we tend to sabotage ourselves. Our insecurity is like a hot button in the center of our hearts, and when someone hits it, we're likely to do anything from having a meltdown to moving to another continent.

We can ask God, "How do you want me to handle this? What is the response you'd like for me to have instead?" For me, when that fear pops up, I've continued to proactively make plans for protecting my relationships and ensuring (as much as I can) that my heart is understood. That usually means setting aside time for a meaningful conversation with one or more people. Most of the time it turns out my fears are unfounded. But it's still worth it both for my peace of mind and because it strengthens bonds with the people I love.

### My Signature Insecurity Strategy

*My signature insecurity is:*

_____

_____

*When that button gets pushed, I usually react this way:*

_____

_____

*With God's help I'm going to try to respond like this instead:*

_____

_____

Changing your reactions takes time. At first, the main goal is simply to recognize when your signature insecurity is at work. Look for fear that seems disproportionate to the actual situation, exceptionally strong emotions, and a desire to do something to make it better *now* (this is often where the sabotaging starts). Then take a moment to say, "Well, there's my old friend the signature insecurity coming to visit me again." Say a quick prayer and think through the response you'd like to choose instead. It can also help to have someone to text or call if you feel overwhelmed and can't get a handle on the situation. Tell them in advance, "I'm going to try to change this pattern in my life, and I need your help. If I text you or call you, please pray. I also give you permission to remind me of my new strategy."

And if you can manage to laugh about it by yourself or with that person, even better. Signature insecurities tell us to take ourselves and our lives way too seriously. Sometimes poking a bit of fun at them can be like popping a balloon. We're all a little nuts in some way. There's not a normal person among us. But we're also incredibly gifted with amazing strengths that can change the world. The more we learn to manage our signature insecurities, the more they can fade to the background so who we really are can shine.

## Spiritual Sabotage: Feeling Guilty

In interviews with Whitney Houston, you can hear the enormous struggle between some of her choices and her faith. Her words are laden with guilt. But that guilt never proved strong enough to make her completely change. That's the illusion of guilt: it makes us feel as if we're going to be different, but ultimately it only discourages us.

In my family, we like to say, "Guilt is the gift that keeps on giving." We share it at the holidays. We pass it around the table like gravy. We heap it up and store it away for future generations. We are good at guilt. We know it and we can laugh about it together.

We're also learning how to get free of it. Because guilt is not really a gift at all. It's a burden—one that we're never meant to carry.

When I talk with women who are experiencing depression or anxiety, they almost all have one factor in common: guilt. The more guilt, the more likely they are to experience negative symptoms both emotionally and physically.

"But wait a minute," you might be thinking. "None of us is perfect. Shouldn't we feel guilty?" The simple, scandalous answer is "Nope."

The author of Hebrews encourages us to "draw near to God with a sincere heart and with the full assurance that faith brings, having our hearts sprinkled to cleanse us from a guilty conscience" (10:22).

This verse appears in a passage explaining to Jewish believers why they no longer need to make sacrifices for their sins. Jesus has come and he has taken their guilt once and for all! The conclusion? "Sacrifice for sin is no longer necessary" (Heb. 10:18).

While we're probably not tempted to go grab a lamb and set up an altar in the backyard every time we sin, I think this passage is still so important for us. Here's what I've come to see: *guilt is the modern-day version of trying to make sacrifices for sins.* We mess up and tell ourselves we have to pay somehow. We sacrifice our joy, our worth, even our fellowship with God to show we are sorry. Then after we've done that for long enough, we feel as if we can move on because we have paid the price for what we've done.

Guilt is about the law.

We are people of grace.

We don't have to sacrifice for our sins anymore. Instead, we can receive what Jesus has done for us. "If we confess our sins, he is faithful and just and will forgive us our sins and purify us from all unrighteousness" (1 John 1:9).

When the author of Hebrews wrote to the Jewish people, the law had expanded far beyond what God originally intended. The

Pharisees had created hundreds of "extra" laws too. So many times when the people were sacrificing, it wasn't even for anything that God had commanded.

We can do the same as well. We often feel "false guilt" for things that God never even asked of us in the first place. In that case, we don't need to ask forgiveness for what we've actually done. Instead, we need to ask forgiveness for putting ourselves under the law in ways that are man-made rather than from God.

While we don't have to bear guilt, we do need conviction in our lives. God doesn't want us to simply run wild. Instead, he asks us to love him, each other, and ourselves. When we fall short of that (and we all do every day), his Holy Spirit is there to remind us of who we are and what we're called to do.

Here's the difference between guilt and conviction:

| Guilt | Conviction |
|---|---|
| ○ Condemns who we are | ○ Calls us back to who we are in Christ |
| ○ Discourages us | ○ Encourages us |
| ○ Leads to negative emotion | ○ Leads to positive change |
| ○ Is about the law | ○ Is about love |
| ○ Makes us sorry | ○ Guides us to repentance |
| ○ Pushes us down | ○ Picks us back up |
| ○ Makes us harsh with others | ○ Teaches us to extend acceptance to others |
| ○ Causes more pain | ○ Brings healing |
| ○ Focuses on us | ○ Points us to Jesus |

Because we're not made for guilt, it's one of the greatest triggers for our self-sabotage. Many times we even become so ashamed of ourselves that we feel it no longer matters what we do. So we give in even more to temptation or accept a lifestyle God never intended for us.

Guilt also sabotages us by being a huge energy drain. Even when we are doing well and trying hard, guilt reminds us of how we've messed up. Our daily lives become not about grace and love but about making up for past mistakes. I've listened to so many women in tears telling me how tired they are because guilt feels like a debt they will never be able to repay. Emotionally, spiritually, and physically, they feel bankrupt.

And what they're saying is true. We can never make up for what we've done. We can never cover our debt. We can never earn God's love. *That's exactly why we need a Savior.* Guilt and all our efforts that come from it can never make us right in God's eyes. But the death of Jesus on the cross can.

When we turn our lives over to him, all our sins are forgiven. And when we mess up (and we will), we can receive more forgiveness. As much as we need.

God loves us too much not to tell our hearts when we need to change. He also loves us too much to let us live with guilt.

Like it's been for me, guilt may be the gift that has kept on giving in your life. If that's the case, friend, it's time to release it to God. Let him take it away forever. What he's got for you is so much better.

## Physical Sabotage: Ignoring Our Bodies

The voice that captivated me as a girl slowly began to fade within Whitney Houston. Drugs, alcohol, and stress began to strip away the gift God had placed inside her. The nature of a gift is that it is entrusted to us, which means we're responsible for caring for it. Yes, that includes the spiritual aspect, but because we are eternal beings in temporary bodies, it involves the physical parts of us as well.

Before we get started, I will tell you that I'm not some super exercise and health nut. I love food. I hate running. I like to say, "I don't work out so I can weigh less. I work out so I can eat more." Yes and amen.

That being said, based on what I've seen as I've worked with many women and observed my life too, it would be impossible for me not to include our bodies here. They are crucial to how we honor God, bless others, and take care of ourselves. My goal here is not to get you on a diet or make you run a marathon. I just want to share some of the amazing ways your body works so you can decide how to best make your body your ally.

Like we've talked about before, what we feel has a physical component. Despite what we often picture, emotions are not invisible things floating around within us somewhere. They are actual chemical reactions. God made us that way.

The feel-good chemicals are called endorphins. They are related to increases in pleasure and decreases in pain. Here's the miracle: our natural endorphins are like built-in antidepressants. We release endorphins when we exercise. Studies have shown that exercise can be just as effective against depression as medication in many cases.

Here's how it works. Movement and growth tell your body you are alive and well. Being sedentary tells your body you are sick or dying. And it responds accordingly. In *Younger Next Year for Women*, Chris Crowley and Dr. Henry Lodge say, "Biologically, there is no such thing as retirement, or even aging. There is only growth or decay. And your body looks to you to choose between them."[2] We've all heard the saying "actions speak louder than words," and nowhere is that truer than in your body. What you do tells your body how to live. You put it on a path to growth—which means health, energy, and joy. Or you put it on a path to decay—which means sickness, exhaustion, and depression. I understand that sometimes we experience health issues beyond our control, and if you're in the middle of that, I'm truly sorry. What we're talking about here is what we *can* control about our physical lives. More and more studies are showing that even those with chronic or serious illness can benefit from lifestyle changes.

So how much exercise does it take? Thirty minutes a day, three times a week is the threshold found to be as effective as antidepressants. But even ten to fifteen minutes can make a difference![3] That's also enough to tell your body that you are on the path to growth and health.

The most effective type of exercise program combines cardio exercise, which works your heart (like running or biking), with strengthening exercise (like lifting weights).

We sabotage ourselves when we limit our capacity to feel joy because we keep our brain from producing the feel-good chemicals God has given to us to get through this life. We may be praying, "God, help me feel better." And he might be saying, "Go for a walk."

I'm not trying to diminish major depression or say that these solutions are simple. If you have mental illness, then you need to get professional, long-term help. I also believe there is a time and place for medication. I have personally struggled with seasons of depression and significant anxiety. What I'm talking about here is more of the everyday ups and downs of life that stress us out.

I also understand that some types of illness may limit our ability to exercise. If that's true of you, talk with your doctor and see what's possible, then together come up with a plan that works for you and your physical circumstances.

Exercise is useful for another purpose besides just managing our emotions and energy levels. It also tells our flesh that it is not in control. The apostle Paul said:

> Do you not know that in a race all the runners run, but only one gets the prize? Run in such a way as to get the

prize. Everyone who competes in the games goes into strict training. They do it to get a crown that will not last, but we do it to get a crown that will last forever. Therefore I do not run like someone running aimlessly; I do not fight like a boxer beating the air. No, I strike a blow to my body and make it my slave so that after I have preached to others, I myself will not be disqualified for the prize. (1 Cor. 9:24–27)

Yes, he's making a spiritual analogy, but I also believe there is some literal, practical truth here too. You have to communicate to your body through your actions that your physical self is not in charge of you—Jesus is. Exercise is one way to do so. It lets us "deny ourselves" in a very real way.

What we eat also acts in the same way. Now, girl, I love a good cupcake as much as anyone. So I'm not going to tell you to give up sugar or eat tofu for every meal. What I do want us to consider together is how what we eat impacts how we feel and our quality of life.

The crash after too much sugar can make us feel tired.

The hangover after too much alcohol can make us feel depressed.

The buzz after too much caffeine can make us feel anxious.

Again, this is not about complete elimination (except in some cases) but instead moderation. Your body is unlike any other. It's up to you to know what makes it feel best and to give it that the majority of the time. Note: What feels good in the moment is often different from what leads to long-term good health.

There's truth to the saying "you are what you eat," because the food and liquids you take in cause chemical reactions in your body. Some for better, others for worse.

I'm not going to linger on this topic because I'm not a physical trainer or a nutritionist. But because I see so many Christian women ignoring this aspect of their lives (and I have done so as well), I couldn't in good conscience write this chapter without mentioning it.

So let's talk about a simple strategy to help you make some changes in the physical aspects of your life. I use the acronym AMISH. (Weird, I know. But it's easy to remember, right?)

- *Awareness*—Simply notice how you feel at different times of the day. Are you hungry, tired, thirsty, moody? If it helps, keep a food diary or write down a number between one and five that rates your mood at various points in the day. Websites and smartphone apps like My Fitness Pal can be really helpful in tracking exercise and what you eat.

- *Movement*—As we talked about, this is really about telling your body that you are healthy and thriving. That means growing your physical wellness a little each day. Make it a goal to do a bit more than you did last week. For example, if you're just beginning to be active, park your car a few spaces farther out at the store. Swap fruit for one sweet treat. *Starting small is always better than not at all.*

- *Integrate*—We tend to separate our spiritual and physical lives. I remember once asking a young girl who had a strong faith yet was struggling with an eating disorder, "How are your faith and your body connected?" She gave me a blank stare and then replied, "They're not." And closing that gap is exactly where we started. Ask God to be involved in taking care of your body just like he is in other parts of your life.

- *Stick with it*—It's easy to make grand plans for exercise and changes in what we eat. Then life interrupts, we go on vacation, or our toddler decides vegetables are evil. So we throw the whole thing out. But just like everything else we learn, finding the healthy lifestyle that really works for us takes a lot of experimentation. If you try something and it doesn't work, try something else. The only exercise program I've ever been able to stick to is riding a stationary bike while I check email on my iPhone. It took me years to figure out my brain has to be occupied or I'll get so bored that I quit.

- *Have fun*—In study after study, research has shown that people stick with what they enjoy. You can only force yourself to do something through sheer willpower for so long. Yes, exercise is not always enjoyable, but what you choose needs to be something you at least like a little. Then eventually the endorphins kick in and help you like it a lot. Find healthy food that tastes good. Do activities with people if you like that better. Again, it's all about experimentation. You know your body better than anyone.

The hardest time of all to keep up the above is when we're stressed. Yet that's when we need it most. I told you to do what's easy and fun, but sometimes we have to bypass that and continue healthy habits because we know it's what we need. In especially stressful times, it's okay to make adjustments, ask for accountability, or do whatever you need to do to persevere.

Your body is a miracle. Your heart beats, your eyes blink, your hair grows without you even thinking about it. Who you are physically reflects the creativity of the One who made you. He gave this body to you. Now you can offer it back to him. "Therefore, I urge you, brothers and sisters, in view of God's mercy, to offer your bodies as a living sacrifice, holy and pleasing to God—this is your true and proper worship" (Rom. 12:1). This brings God great joy—and he's physically made you so that it does the same for you!

## From Sabotage to Support

Whitney Houston never made peace with the one person who might have been able to save her life: herself. While there are still debates over what exactly led to her destructive decline, even Whitney herself said she played a role in it.

My heart aches when I think about her because we are not that different. We are all capable of sabotaging ourselves. While it may not cost us our lives, it can easily cost us our joy, peace, relationships, and health.

On the flip side, it doesn't have to be that way. We are just as capable of supporting ourselves as we are of being saboteurs. In fact, we're commanded to love ourselves. Jesus said, "Love your neighbor *as yourself*" (Matt. 22:39, emphasis added).

Paul poses this question: "If God is for us, who can be against us?" (Rom. 8:31). The answer should be "no one," but there is one person who can be: you. When we come against ourselves, we side with the enemy.

Be on God's side. And on your side. You are a beautiful, wonderfully created woman with gifts to offer this world. You make a difference more than you know. You are called by God and have a purpose that is beyond what you can even imagine. He has a good plan for you, and with him you are unstoppable.

So go for it, friend, and let nothing stand in your way—not even you.

# 6

# You're Made for a **Promised Land**

Now the LORD God had planted a garden in the east, in Eden; and there he put the man he had formed. The LORD God made all kinds of trees grow out of the ground—trees that were pleasing to the eye and good for food. In the middle of the garden were the tree of life and the tree of the knowledge of good and evil. A river watering the garden flowed from Eden.

Genesis 2:8–10

For the LORD your God is bringing you into a good land—a land with brooks, streams, and deep springs gushing out into the valleys and hills; a land with wheat and barley, vines and fig trees, pomegranates, olive oil and honey; a land where bread will not be scarce and

you will lack nothing; a land where the rocks are iron
and you can dig copper out of the hills. When you have
eaten and are satisfied, praise the LORD your God for
the good land he has given you.

Deuteronomy 8:7–10

Then the angel showed me the river of the water of
life, as clear as crystal, flowing from the throne of God
and of the Lamb down the middle of the great street of
the city. On each side of the river stood the tree of life,
bearing twelve crops of fruit, yielding its fruit every
month. And the leaves of the tree are for the healing
of the nations. No longer will there be any curse. The
throne of God and of the Lamb will be in the city, and
his servants will serve him. They will see his face.

Revelation 22:1–4

Our story begins in a perfect garden.

It takes us to a Promised Land.

It ends with a new heaven and earth.

The heartbeat of God for his people doesn't change from Genesis to Revelation. It's clear he wants us to thrive. He longs to bless us, yearns to bring us joy, stops at nothing to make sure we have an opportunity to experience life to the full.

Somewhere along the line it seems we've gotten a bit confused. At least I have. I believed for many years that the Christian life was all about suffering. But as I look through the pages of Scripture, I just can't find that to be true.

Yes, we are told we will have trouble and hard times. We will grieve. We will face loss. We will be disappointed.

But those places of pain are not where we're made to *dwell*. Think back to those three passages at the beginning. They're places God intended his people to be long term. Adam and Eve sinned and lost the garden. The people of Israel rebelled and spent forty years in the desert, then did the same in the Promised Land and got exiled. Some people will choose to reject God and therefore forfeit heaven. But *his* plan is for us to live in good lands. The words associated with those places aren't temporary ones—they are words like *possess, dwell, live,* and *forever.*

In contrast, when God talks about tough places, the words are temporary. In particular, God uses the word *through* again and again. For example, the Israelites passed *through* the Red Sea. They passed *through* the desert. They eventually passed *through* the Jordan and into the Promised Land.

Perhaps Isaiah 43:2 expresses it best:

> When you pass through the waters,
>     I will be with you;
> and when you pass through the rivers,
>     they will not sweep over you.
> When you walk through the fire,
>     you will not be burned;
>     the flames will not set you ablaze.

Why does this matter? Because if we believe God doesn't want us to have a good life, then we will stay in places he never intended. We will settle for less than he has for us. We will make hard times our identity rather than a stop along the way.

I'm not saying that life will be easy. Jesus said, "In this world you will have trouble," yet he also followed it with, "But take heart! I have overcome the world" (John 16:33). Let's make sure we don't let false beliefs add to the pain we will inevitably experience in this world. You are made for a Promised Land.

............

# Yes, You're Allowed to Be Happy

I sit across from my friend at breakfast. Over coffee and bagels, I whisper a confession: "My life is good, but sometimes I'm still not happy." I think of all the blessings I've been given. I know I should be grateful. *And yet.* There's this nagging sense that I'm falling short of life to the full. My friend clears her throat and responds that she too struggles with the idea of happiness.

Stories of how to survive struggles abound. Books about depression and hard times line the shelves of local stores.

But happiness?

Life to the full?

We giggle like schoolgirls because it almost feels like we're talking about a taboo subject. Isn't happiness selfish and, well, worldly?

My friend and I talk about how happiness—not just joy—appears throughout Scripture. We speak of the world around us and how there's so much that seems to be here simply for our enjoyment. We agree that, yes, happiness is certainly not to be our primary aim in life. But isn't it supposed to be part of our faith journey?

Eden.

The Promised Land.

Heaven.

I finally get the courage to ask the question that has been lingering in the back of my mind for a long time: "Are we allowed to be happy?"

And if so, how do we make happiness happen the way God intends?

I have to know.

That question sends me on a journey I never expected. I study brain science. I speak with counseling clients. I get certified as a life coach. I hear from the hearts of thousands of women. I study verse after verse.

As I do, a pattern begins to emerge. You could even call it a map. And the answer to my question is clear: yes, not only are we allowed to be happy, but God desires for us to experience a life of well-being.

God is not the cosmic killjoy many of us imagine. All of the evidence points to the opposite. We serve a God of joy, abundance, blessings, and fullness. "The LORD be exalted, who delights in the well-being of his servant" (Ps. 35:27). He wants us to thrive.

Like any good father, he experiences joy when his children do too. "May the righteous be glad and rejoice before God; may they be happy and joyful" (Ps. 68:3).

But there's a catch. Happiness doesn't just happen. It's not something we can sit around and wait to receive. It's not automatic—quite the opposite. We are fallen people living in a broken world, and happiness is something we must be intentional about if we're to experience it. In many ways, happiness takes hard work.

Even joy requires our openness and being willing to receive it. And it's a choice we have to make every single day. A part of life to the full we have to fight for sometimes.

But it is worth it.

Months later, my friend and I meet again for breakfast. I slide into the booth with a smile. "I found the answer," I say. "Happiness is allowed—and possible for all of us."

She leans across the table and says, "Tell me more."

So I do.

And now I want to do the same for you.

## Myths That Hold Us Back

It turns out what holds many of us back from experiencing joy and happiness are myths that we've believed.

### Myth #1: The Promised Land Is Only in Heaven

I've been to a few funerals in my lifetime. I imagine you have as well. While the lives of those being honored vary widely, it seems the language that comes from the clergyman delivering the message is often similar. At some point, there's usually a mention of "crossing the Jordan" and entering the Promised Land. I've heard the same kind of wording from the pulpit for years. One day I wondered, "Is that really true? Do we have to wait until death to reach the Promised Land?"

I flipped through the pages of my Bible until I found the story of the Israelites finally crossing the Jordan River into the Promised Land. What followed their entry didn't seem like a prototype of heaven to me. Yes, they were in the land God had given them, but there were still battles to fight, houses to build, laws to follow. Moses gives the people an intricate plan from God for enjoying life to the full in the place where God is taking them.

The more I looked at Scripture, the more I became convinced: the Promised Land isn't just a representation of heaven. Instead, it's what God wants all of us to experience in this life when we live in faithful obedience to him. Yes, the *ultimate* Promised Land (what Scripture symbolically refers to as Zion) is indeed ours when we at last stand in God's presence. But to limit it to that is to miss so much of what God has for us in the here and now.

We began our story in the Garden of Eden. Then God moved his people to the Promised Land, a place "flowing with milk and honey" (Exod. 3:8). Finally, we'll be called home to heaven, which is described as incredibly wonderful as well. It's clear that the desire of God's heart is for us to dwell in the fullness of all he has for us.

The exile of Adam and Eve from Eden, the trek of the Israelites across the desert, the fallen world we live in now—these were never part of God's original intent.

Will we go through deserts and hard times? Yes, we certainly will. Even Jesus, who is perfect, didn't avoid difficulties in his time on earth. But as we talked about, there is a distinct difference between going through trouble and *living* there.

Because of the myth that the only Promised Land is in heaven, it seems many Christians accept the desert as home—as the way it has to be. But that's not true. You are not made for the desert. I'm not made for the desert. God has so much more in store for us, and we don't have to wait until we die to begin receiving it!

This isn't about our outward circumstances. "Though outwardly we are wasting away, yet inwardly we are being renewed day by day" (2 Cor. 4:16). Research has shown that what's happening in our lives usually doesn't have the impact we believe it will. For example, in a study of two groups of people—one that won the lottery and the other that became paralyzed from the neck down—both returned to the basic point of happiness they had before these events after a relatively brief amount of time.[1] The gift God offers is an *internal Promised Land* no matter what our external reality may be.

Jesus said, "I have come that they may have life, and have it to the full" (John 10:10). He didn't say an easy life. He didn't say a self-indulgent life where all your wishes are granted. He didn't say a life free from pain. But he did say a *full* life. One of joy, peace, love, and hope. It's not only possible—it's *promised*. It doesn't come from outward circumstances but instead comes from the Holy Spirit within us. This time we don't dwell in the Promised Land; instead, the Promised One dwells in us. That means we can have life to the full *wherever we are*.

We don't have to wait until we die to begin to really live.

## Myth #2: Happiness Is Selfish

Karen brushes a stray hair from her face as she peers into the mirror. She looks weary and a little worn around the edges. She knows that she should take better care of herself, but doing so seems self-centered. "As long as I'm a good wife and mom, that's all that matters," she tells herself as she steps out of the bathroom and into another day of just surviving.

Women are wonderful givers. We're there to offer a helping hand, lend an ear, or be a shoulder to cry on at a moment's notice. This is a beautiful part of who we are. And yet when we give, give, give with the belief that anything else is selfish, we set ourselves up for burnout.

Author Gretchen Rubin says, "Studies show that happier people are more likely to help other people. They're more interested in social problems. They do more volunteer work and contribute more to charity. Plus, as you'd expect, they're less preoccupied with their personal problems."[2]

Over and over again, research has proven that the happier you are, the *more* likely you are to help others.

Somewhere along the line we've adopted the idea that for others to win, we have to lose. Yet it simply isn't true. And that's not the way God has set up the world to work. Over and over, we're given commands that contain two very important words we've talked about already: *one another*. Those are reciprocal words—they involve giving *and* receiving.

Yes, Jesus gave his all for us. But he asks for us to give our all to him in return too. Hebrews 12:2 says we are to live "fixing our eyes on Jesus, the pioneer and perfecter of faith. *For the joy set before him* he endured the cross, scorning its shame, and sat down at the right hand of the throne of God" (emphasis added). He didn't go to the cross to make the ultimate sacrifice and then be depressed forever. No, Jesus could see the joy on the other side, and it enabled him to push through and do what needed to be done. The idea that we are to endlessly suffer as a way to be selfless simply doesn't line up with biblical truth.

*Happiness will not make you selfish.* Instead, it will most likely do just the opposite—allow you to serve even more out of an overflow.

## Myth #3: Joy Has to Be Earned

I wish I could knock on your door or stop by your space, tap you on the shoulder, and say, "I've got a gift for you." I'd hand you a package wrapped with a bow.

You'd ask, "For me?" with a smile.

I'd nod, grinning. Then you'd slip off the paper and peer inside to see one word: *joy.*

That's what's on my heart for you today, friend.

*More JOY.*

A friend of mine and I prayed together last night—uncovering lies in my life, finding healing, doing some heart work that I deeply needed. Through that process I realized I'd always believed something untrue: that *joy has to be earned.*

When I'm good enough, productive enough, and everyone else is okay, then I can have joy.

The truth?

Joy is a gift just like grace.

You hold the box in your hands, lift the lid again, and peer inside one more time.

"Are you sure you want me to have this?" you ask.

And it seems we both hear a voice beyond words, whispering to our hearts, "Oh yes—and there's plenty more where it came from!"

Joy is something we receive—not something we earn. Yet that doesn't mean it's a passive process. Even when it comes to gifts, there's still action required on our part. We have to be willing to take what's being offered, open it up, and enjoy it.

The first step to doing so is usually stopping to recognize that we don't have to *deserve* joy. It's a fruit of the Spirit. It's a gift to us as children of God. It's part of our Promised Land. Joy isn't about being perfect. It's about being perfectly loved.

Yes, sin and rebellion steal our joy. But that's different from simply feeling unworthy and therefore not allowing ourselves to feel joy. You have been made worthy through Jesus and his sacrifice on the cross. We don't have to earn our joy because it has already been paid for in full.

## Myth #4: There's Always More Time

I sit in the bleachers on Friday night as sun and storm clouds play tag over a stadium. My beautiful niece will soon walk across the stage to receive her diploma. As students wait, hands on their caps to keep the wind from stealing them, my husband points to glints of light on the other side of the fence. "What's that?" he asks.

We both squint toward the odd shapes stretched out across a green patch of grass. I finally realize what they are. "It's a cemetery," I say.

For the rest of the night my eyes drift between students beginning the next chapter of their lives and the markers of some who have closed the last chapter (in this life, anyway).

It seems I hear echoes as the valedictorian talks of making each moment count, being sure you change the world, having one life to live.

The years between that walk across the stage and the walk into eternity will fly by. You and I—we're somewhere in the middle. So lean in and listen to this . . .

*You are the only you we will ever have. God didn't create a plan B for your life. We need you to be who you are, to do what only you can do. And to do it now, today, in whatever way you can.*

We live our lives waiting for the big moments—the "walk across the stage" times in life. But those are few and far between.

I think the folks who have completed the journey would say instead that it's the little moments that really matter. The ones you think aren't important. The ones you wish you could skip.

But those moments? They're life.

Make the most of them.

My niece crosses the stage. We cheer as loud as we can.

*Joy.*

And I wonder, just wonder, if the same happens often in heaven too. Perhaps it does every time we take a step of faith until we cross that final stage. Not because of how big we are but because it shows how BIG our God is.

Do you think angels ever say, "Woo-hoo"?

> Therefore, since we are surrounded by such a great cloud of witnesses, let us throw off everything that hinders and the sin that so easily entangles. And let us run with perseverance the race marked out for us, fixing our eyes on Jesus, the pioneer and perfecter of faith. For the joy set before him he endured the cross, scorning its shame, and sat down at the right hand of the throne of God. (Heb. 12:1–2)

............

We tend to believe we'll always have more time. But life passes by quickly. We trade joy and happiness for a string of "When I's," only to discover that those never come or they're quickly replaced by another condition. We don't know how long we have here, but we can be certain it's not forever. I love how King David says, "*This* is the day the LORD has made; we will rejoice and be glad in it" (Ps. 118:24 NKJV, emphasis added). He doesn't say, "Yesterday was the day the Lord made" or "Tomorrow is the day the Lord will make." Instead, he focuses on what's right in front of us. The here and now. As is.

We may not know how much time we have, but we always have time for joy. It's right there in front of us, in this moment, and the God who so graciously gives it to us is too.

## Myth #5: I Should Be Happy All the Time

I tossed and turned in bed, then stared at the ceiling. Discontent circled my thoughts and landed on various areas of my life—relationships, work, spirituality. I alternated between picturing the ideal in each of those areas and looking at the "real." What I actually experienced from day to day differed from what I'd like to have as my life. I wound up feeling like a failure, wishing for different circumstances, and dreading the coming of another day.

As I silently whispered a prayer for help, a realization slowly began to come to my heart: I had a false expectation that I should be happy all the time. I treated those ideal scenarios as standards to meet rather than impossibilities this side of heaven. I was shocked to discover that the surest way to make sure you don't have happiness or joy in your life is to demand it.

When I expected happiness or my idea of "perfection" in my life, it made me overlook the blessings that were actually right in front of me. I didn't stop to thank God for all I had. Instead, I continually pushed for more, more, more. If you had asked me, I would have described this as part of being godly. But underneath what I thought was true I came to see that really I was demanding life on my terms. I couldn't give up control. And because I couldn't give up control, I couldn't receive. And if you can't receive, you can't experience happiness or joy.

(Ouch. It hurt to write those words!)

But staying in that place of discontent hurt even more. As I considered how I'd actually blocked my happiness by demanding it, I felt the breath slowly slip from my lungs. Peace washed over me in that moment of quietness. I hadn't realized how much pressure all of those "ideals" had been putting on my life. No wonder I felt stressed out and anxious a lot of the time! I was carrying a burden God never intended.

We live in a fallen, broken world. Things are never going to be exactly as we wish. The sooner we realize that and can accept it, the sooner we can begin to find the joy in what we've actually been given.

My dear friend Sara Frankl spent the last several years of her life confined to her home because of illness. She knew that much of what most of us would consider part of "normal" life would be impossible for her. Stripped of those expectations, Sara became one of the most joyful people I've ever met. She described herself this way:

> I'm just a girl who used to write for a magazine to make a living, and now writes a blog to make a life. Extremely blessed, well-loved, and choosing joy while learning that homebound doesn't limit your life, just your location. I hope you find something on here that makes you smile or makes you think. Or both.[3]

Sara's motto was "Choose joy," and that's what she did until Jesus took her home.

Sara discovered a secret that few of us know: we can sabotage our good lives by demanding perfect ones. Our pursuit of happiness can actually be the very thing that keeps it forever out of our grasp.

Hebrews 13:5 says, "Be content with what you have, because God has said, 'Never will I leave you; never will I forsake you.'" You have what's essential. In the story of Mary and Martha, two sisters live very differently. Martha bustles about trying to make things "as they should be." Mary sits at the feet of a Savior who is everything she truly needs. Jesus speaks truth to Martha when he says, "Mary has chosen what is better, and it will not be taken away from her" (Luke 10:42). Everything in our lives is either out of our grasp or can be taken from us. Everything but Jesus. That's a hard truth to hear—but it's a truth that can set us free from the illusion that if we just tried harder, earned more, or prayed longer, then we could have the life we imagine.

Life is hard. Happiness is found not through escaping that reality but by embracing it. The bars that lock us away from joy may be of our own making.

Dare to find the joy where you are now. Dare to drop your expectations. Dare to believe that only one thing in your life can be perfect—and that is the One who gave it to you.

*Which of these myths may have been holding you back?*

_____

_____

## What If You're Still Stuck?

Because we're complex people, living in joy is not as simple as telling yourself to do it. We all face times when getting "through" seems like just too much to do. If you feel like you are stuck, then it's time to get some help. Let's look at some ways that folks in Scripture did the same.

*Don't go it alone*—The journey into the Promised Land was not done one person at a time. It happened in community. Even when Adam was in the Garden of Eden, God said, "It is not good for the man to be alone" (Gen. 2:18). It's not a sign of weakness to need help. Actually, reaching out is inner strength displayed. Find someone to support you during this time. If you are facing depression or anxiety that is severe enough to interfere with your daily life, choose someone who is gifted and trained to deal with those things, such as a licensed counselor. You can find a counselor in your area by going to www.ecounseling.com.

*Be willing to risk*—When the Israelites left Egypt, God parted the Red Sea, and they had to walk through it as a step of faith. When they reached the Jordan River just before the Promised Land, he had them do the same. It wasn't until the priests actually stepped into the water that God did a miracle. Sometimes fear is what's holding us back. When that's true and we know what God has asked us to do, obedience is the only way through to the other side. And here's the thing: the fear isn't going away. You've just gotta do it anyway. One small step at a time.

*Keep God first*—Over and over, the Israelites chose to rebel against the Lord. First they wandered in the desert, and then they were exiled from the Promised Land. When Moses explained what the people were to obey, he said:

> Hear, Israel, and be careful to obey so that it may go well with you and that you may increase greatly in a land flowing with milk and honey, just as the LORD, the God of your ancestors, promised you. Hear, O Israel: The LORD our God, the LORD is one. Love the LORD your God with all your heart and with all your soul and

with all your strength. These commandments that I give you today are to be on your hearts. (Deut. 6:3–6)

Not all hard times are because of sin or rebellion; often they are simply the result of living in a fallen world. But obedience is essential to living in joy long term.

*When you mess up, move back toward the Promised Land*—Y'all, the chart below changed my life. And you know I mean it because I don't bring out the Southern accent unless I'm serious.

## Promised Land
### Moderation, Joy

## Desert
### Deprivation

## Exile
### Overindulgence

Sometimes it can be hard to determine how God really wants us to live. But in every area, every decision, it seems as believers we have three places we can end up through our choices: desert, Promised Land, or exile. The Israelites ended up wandering the desert for forty years and exiled from the Promised Land for four hundred for the same reason: disobedience. But the kind of rebellion was very different. In the desert, they refused to receive what God had for them. They deprived themselves of the blessings God wanted to bestow. Once in the Promised Land, they misused the abundant blessings God gave to them and were sent into exile. We probably lean more toward one type of rebellion than the other. If we tend to rebel like those in the desert, we may be legalistic and resist receiving what God has for us. If we're more like those who got exiled, we do whatever feels good and take whatever we want.

(Note: Throughout this section I'm talking about specific disobedient choices we willfully make and *not* about hard times that come to us such as loss or grief. Those are completely different and not related to rebellion.)

God's desire is for us to dwell in the Promised Land. That means we receive what he says is good, and we practice self-control through the Spirit as we do. When we live this way, we're showing God we love him, and we reap great benefits. "Be careful to obey so that it may go well with you and that you may increase greatly in a land flowing with milk and honey, just as the LORD, the God of your ancestors, promised you" (Deut. 6:3).

For example, let's talk through our relationship with food. In the desert, we deprive ourselves. We won't enjoy what God has given. We never feel thin enough. When we head toward exile, we consistently gorge on food to make it fill places (like our hearts) it was never intended to fill. In the Promised Land, we enjoy God's gift of food in a way that's healthy overall and also increases our capacity to feel joy.

If we're talking about sex, then the desert would be saying that sex is bad and dirty, so therefore we shouldn't really enjoy it even in God-ordained ways. Moving toward exile would be giving in to lust and indulging our flesh in sin. The Promised Land would be celebrating our sexuality and seeing it as a gift from God that we share with our spouse.

*What is an area of struggle in your life?*

*Where are you with it right now? Place a dot on the chart below to represent it.*

## Promised Land
Moderation, Joy

## Desert
Deprivation

## Exile
Overindulgence

*What's one change you need to ask God to help you make so that you move closer to what he has for you?*

_____

_____

We will all struggle. Thankfully, we are under grace and so we can always ask for God's help to get us back to where we really belong.

*Fight for joy*—As we talked about earlier, joy doesn't come naturally to us. It's something we have to make a practice of and return to again and again. But God takes joy very seriously. When the Israelites were about to enter the Promised Land, he warned them of the curses that would come upon them if they rebelled. One of the things he mentioned specifically as rebellion? "Because you did not serve the LORD your God joyfully and gladly in the time of prosperity" (Deut. 28:47). Solomon, considered the wisest king who ever lived, said, "I know that there is nothing better for people than to be happy and to do good while they live. That each of them may eat and drink, and find satisfaction in all their toil—this is the gift of God" (Eccles. 3:12–13). The apostle Paul admonished early believers, "Rejoice in the Lord always" (Phil. 4:4).

When hard things happen and losses come into your life, grieve for as long as you need to heal. It's okay to feel frustration. It's normal to be disappointed. Sometimes you will even just have a bad day for no reason at all. All of that is part of being human. This isn't about being happy all the time but is about consistently finding your way back to joy. If you can't ever do so, that's a warning sign that you need help from someone else like a counselor (and I believe we all do at times). Make a commitment that when you pass through hard times, you will not dwell in them—whatever it takes.

## Don't Settle

I'm sitting in a busy café and can't help but hear a conversation between two friends. Finally, one remarks, "All I'm saying is, don't settle." The other girl smiles because she knows what her friend really means is, "I love you and I want the very best for you." And if you were across a table from me, I'd say the same to you right now.

Don't settle in the desert.

Don't settle in the hard places.

Don't settle in depression.

Don't settle in fear.

Don't settle anywhere but in the center of all God has for you.

You aren't created to settle. You're created to dwell.

"Surely your goodness and love will follow me all the days of my life, and I will dwell in the house of the Lord forever" (Ps. 23:6).

You really are made for a Promised Land.

# 7

# You'll **Remember** These Words

I wander through the house and peek at surfaces, reach into bags, ask my husband what he's seen. "Where did I put those sunglasses?" I wonder as I lift a hand to scratch my head. And, of course, there they are, perched neatly atop my very blonde hair. I giggle. Sometimes our minds are forgetful.

I wander through my thoughts, peek at old memories, reach into lessons learned, ask my friends their opinions. "Where did I put that truth I need right now?" I wonder as I place a shaking hand across my chest. And, of course, suddenly it's there—the words I need to make it through the day, whispered from God to me. I grin. Sometimes our hearts are forgetful too.

I'm in a place of needing to remind my heart of what's real, what's true, what I can hold on to forever. Maybe you are too?

It seems we especially need those reminders when we're dealing with stress, a bad day, or a hard time. So let's take some time to remember the things our hearts forget.

Truth doesn't ever go anywhere. But sometimes we lose what we know in the middle of the busy or the hard. Thankfully, we can always go back and what we need is right there waiting for us. As close as the sunglasses we discover are already on our heads.

I hope you'll remember these words with the same feeling of joy and relief I had when I touched those sunglasses and said, "Oh yes, that's right! There's what I need!"

## Things Our Hearts Forget: You're Seen

The sun slips behind the spring trees exploding green. The birds declare love and war from the tips of branches. My dog stares down a squirrel, daring it to take one more step along the fence. The fire pit is just beginning to crackle to life, sparks of gold and orange scattering into ashes.

I lean back in the rocking chair and find a rhythm that matches my thoughts. I feel small today. Like one of the sparrows scurrying across the yard. Back and forth. Back and forth. It's hard to see what all the fuss is about.

Then I remember that just as I see that sparrow, I'm seen too. By a God who made me. Knows me. Calls my name above the treetops and within my heart. Yes, I'm small.

*But in God's eyes, size doesn't equal significance.*

The One who spun the stars onto the floor of the sky like dancers in evening gowns does not consider me of little importance. The One who watches seeds sleep beneath the earth and then unfold into glory has a different point of view.

I matter to him.

You do too.

We are not unseen.

Not now. ·

Not ever.

"For the eyes of the LORD range throughout the earth to strengthen those whose hearts are fully committed to him" (2 Chron. 16:9).

I let the night fall around me like a curtain, watch the fire drift away in slivers of smoke. I am invisible, hidden, small. And at the same time fully seen, known, given significance beyond what I can even grasp.

I rock in my chair to the rhythm of this paradox until my heart does the same. Then I fully surrender to the unexpected sway of joy.

## Things Our Hearts Forget: Your Works Don't Equal Your Worth

My hands roll dough across the counter. I'm conquering one of my greatest fears: cinnamon rolls from scratch.

How can I be so intimidated by yeast and flour, sugar and butter, the thick, stretchy dough that begins to lengthen and take form beneath my hands?

I realize, slowly, that it's not about the dough at all. *It's about what I believe the outcome will say about me.*

There's some part of me that believes my worth is somehow tied to my ability to make decent cinnamon rolls. It sounds ridiculous, I know, but it's only one in a string of many such expectations I carry.

*I must be able to decorate my house.*

*I must be able to accessorize.*

*I must be able to make coherent small talk.*

You can write your own list.

But what it all comes down to is believing this: *you're only as good as what you can produce.* And that, my friends, is a sure way to drive yourself crazy.

I slap the dough with my bare hands, roll it across more flour. It resists and I don't blame it.

If my worth does not come from what I produce, then where does it come from?

I realize slowly as the flour shifts that my worth is not something *I can make.* It's not cinnamon rolls. Or a tidy house. Or the perfect outfit.

It's a gift. Offered with outstretched hands by the One who *made me.*

I don't produce my worth. I receive it.

And then, in joy and love, I live it out . . . maybe even sometimes by making cinnamon rolls.

The dough yields at last. I cut it into circles, load it into pans, bake it into goodness.

When I finally take a bite, I taste cinnamon, butter, sugar.

And grace.

Yes, an extra sprinkling of grace.

## Things Our Hearts Forget: Your Secrets and Struggles Don't Disqualify You

The walkway to our house is trimmed in vibrant green on a backdrop of black mulch. Emeralds on velvet. I stroll past the familiar leaves of the plants that return all on their own.

My favorites, two chubby hostas, like to tease us. Every year we wonder if perhaps winter got them, and then at the last moment, they pop out of the ground like smiling children.

Other more sinister green always appears too. Weeds that sneak into corners and burrow into shadows until we find them. They're like secrets in this garden. When we come across one, my husband declares, "Weed!" and yanks it sternly from the roots. A swift and efficient extraction.

For some reason, the weeds always surprise me. Every year I somehow think our yard will miraculously be free of them. They're not on my mind when we plant, water, and comment on the growth.

But they never surprise my husband. He's known they're somewhere beneath, just waiting for their chance at light and air so they can make an appearance.

He would never decide not to plant flowers because of the weeds that would come too. And when he finds the weeds, he never says, "I knew I shouldn't have planted those flowers!" *The nature of growth is that it comes with weeds.*

Our hearts are much the same. A sin or struggle pops up in our lives and we're horrified. "Oh no!" we declare. "Now everything God has done in my life is ruined!" But God is only interested in pulling the weed. It's not a surprise to him. It doesn't change the beauty he's creating in our lives. It doesn't cancel out the growth we've seen.

God knew all along the weed was there. Now it's simply time to deal with it.

He chose you knowing that seed would one day sprout and come to the surface. And in his infinite love, he picked the perfect time to bring it to your attention so he can remove it.

My husband tosses the weed over his shoulder. I watch it sink out of sight into the trash can. I turn and look at my man, a smile of pride across his face. The weed has already been forgotten. He says, "Don't you think the hostas look especially good this year?"

I glance down at the green, a few stray bits of dirt the only indication of where the weed had so recently been.

I nod my head and agree. "Yes, they're more beautiful than ever."

## Things Our Hearts Forget: Your Sensitivity Can Be a Strength

I yank my arm back from the stove with a yelp. "Ow!" A thin pink line slips across my forearm. Sliding muffins into the oven, I'd gotten a little too close. I seek the sink and run cold water on the heat. A few tears flow too.

As I stand there, I think back over words spoken that slashed across my heart just like the heat of the oven. That place within me still feels tender. I berate myself. "Why am I so sensitive?"

I glance back at my arm, and suddenly I'm thankful for sensitivity. Without it, the burn would have been much worse. And without the sensitivity of my heart, a relationship I value could have been more deeply damaged too.

*Never apologize for your sensitivity.*

Yet don't abuse it either. Being burned didn't mean I should kick the dog or destroy the stove. It didn't give me the right to light a match and go after the next person who crossed my path so they could have a little fire ruin their day too.

We need to let ourselves cry, feel the anger, recognize that we've been burned. It's the way we keep ourselves alive to all that's around us. *First we feel, then we heal.*

I hold a muffin in my hand. Its soothing warmth reaches all the way to my fingertips, to somewhere deep inside.

# Things Our Hearts Forget: You're Not a Quitter

"Let's go!" my spandex-clad husband cheerfully declares as we round a corner on our bikes. I've been enthusiastically pedaling along with him, but suddenly my eyes see it: THE HILL.

"Did we make a wrong turn?" I ask with hope in my voice. His sprint to the base of the incline serves as my answer.

I start strong.

By halfway up I think I might die.

By two-thirds up I'm hoping I will.

I wave farewell to the caterpillar racing past my tire.

The scenes of my life flash before my eyes, and I notice a lot of them contain chocolate.

Then suddenly . . . I'm there.

At the top.

I would whoop and holler with joy, except I can't breathe. But I do manage a lopsided grin. And my husband says, "Aren't you glad you didn't quit?" Despite a strong desire to smack him on his spandex-covered tush for putting me through this, I have to admit he's right. Stinking hill. It was worth it after all.

You will want to quit. More than once.

And fear is always at the root of it.

*I'm not going to make it.*

*I can't do this.*

*It's too much.*

But listen here—you can do it. You're stronger than you know. Your God is bigger than you've seen. That hill isn't as unending as it seems right now.

Just keep *going and going and going.* Until you leave fear and trouble in the dust.

Here's the secret: you're not a quitter . . . you're a climber. You just may not know it yet.

## Things Our Hearts Forget: You're Made to Celebrate

We slide into the last four empty seats on the patio. Red umbrellas wave in welcome as they hover above couples on dates, co-workers winding down, and groups of friends gathered to catch up. My friend Stephanie Bryant and I are here with our husbands for a different reason.

We're here to celebrate. We've just finished a business project. We don't yet know how it will turn out. We've only seen glimpses. We're exhausted.

*But we're celebrating anyway.*

Because after years of creativity and work we've learned this: we're to celebrate God's goodness and our obedience—not results.

The moment you say yes to God and move forward into what he asks of you is the moment you become successful. Not when you hit the numbers. Not when you meet expectations. Not when you make heads turn.

True success happens when no one is looking, when no one hears, in the quiet of your heart where there's only a divine invitation and an acceptance of it.

We feast under a clear blue sky that smells like just-after-rain. The pavement is still wet in some places. There are clouds in the distance. Who knows if they will come our way.

But for now we make time stand still. We don't ask, "What's next?" We don't say, "We really should have . . ." We hold our God-sized dream in our hands and we drink deeply of it. And we feel the delight of the One who gave it to us.

Time ticks again and problems arise, disappointments come, and we're glad we did this first. Before all that. Because it reminds us of what matters.

We need celebration because it covers our souls, like a red umbrella. Joy stretched out above us, held by unseen hands.

## Things Our Hearts Forget: You're Made for Rest

I skid my toes along the edge of the water. It's brilliant blue, the color of the deepest sky. I let out my breath slowly and close my eyes. I listen to the waves. In. Out. In. Out. I match their rhythm and slow down inside.

I think of words spoken by my life coach and friend, Denise Martin. "Holley," she said, "people aren't made to keep the same level of productivity all the time. It comes in waves. Go with it. You need rest sometimes."

I watch the ebb and flow of the tide and know she's right. I've known this somewhere deep inside every time I've come to the ocean since I was a little girl. But I forget. In the middle of the busy and expected, it gets lost.

We are not machines. Only machines can produce nonstop. And even then, they break down.

Rest is not wasted time.

Rest is preparation.

When it's quiet in my life, when I can't hear God's voice, when I can't see the next adventure, I begin to think something is wrong with me. I try to raise the tide. Surely if I can just do something, then I will prove my worth again.

But the God of the sea whispers instead to my heart . . .

*"Peace, child, you are loved."*

*"Peace, child, you are right in the middle of my purpose for you."*
*"Peace, child, more will come when it is time."*

I let those words wash over me again and again until my heart knows their rhythm. Yes, this is the way it is meant to be. Work and rest. Rest and work. And love in it all.

I throw a small shell into the water. It sinks to the bottom, and I watch it resting there, wondering where the waves will take it next. *The inevitable journey.*

And there is no more reason to strive.

## Things Our Hearts Forget: You Have Something to Offer

Sixteen food trucks circle the wide-open field. I read the locations on their sides: Buffalo, Toronto, New York City. Over miles and across borders, these folks have brought what they have to offer. And as I bite into a chocolate-hazelnut cupcake, I smile because we're clearly all benefiting.

I like the idea of food trucks. Wherever you go, you have something to offer. And in case you didn't know, you're kinda like a food truck in that way.

We're all called to feed the hearts around us. "Give us today *our* daily bread," says the line in the Lord's Prayer (Matt. 6:11, emphasis added). What we receive isn't just for us.

And it isn't just for one particular place.

Wherever you are right now, you're bringing what God has given you to offer along with you.

Your home.

Your office.

Your church.

Your community.

Across the world.

It's not just when we sit in a pew on Sunday. It's not just when we're in front of our keyboards writing. It's not just when we're volunteering or going out of our way to make a difference.

*It's all the time, everywhere, just as you are.*

I don't know what you've got inside—what your version of a food truck might be. But I can tell you this: it's going to meet a need. Because God put it there.

So roll down the road of life and see where he takes you. And when someone with a hungry heart crosses your path and God calls, fling open the doors and hold out your hands.

Then trust that whatever has been entrusted to you is what's needed in that moment. And that it's good.

Chocolate-hazelnut cupcake good.

## Things Our Hearts Forget: You're Safe Even outside Your Comfort Zone

I sit in the car, hands wrapped around the steering wheel.

"Holley," my friend says with a smile, "you have to get out of the car."

I sigh. She's right. I am leading the retreat, after all. Wandering into the lobby, I glance at the faces of some women. Some smile, others chat, and a few look as nervous as I feel.

I've come to a lodge to spend the weekend with a women's ministry. And (confession) I'm scared silly.

Have you ever felt afraid even though you knew with all your heart you were supposed to do something? I've found there is only one cure for that kind of fear: do it anyway.

Some fear you can't push down. *You can only go through it.*

By the end of the weekend I had fallen in love with those women. And by the time I grasped the steering wheel again, I felt sad to leave. I couldn't imagine why I'd been so nervous.

Sometimes our comfort zones are the walls that block us from God's best for our lives. When we dare to step beyond them, we open doors to things we never thought possible.

We grow. And our faith does too. Even when life is stressful or scary.

It seems that's where I most often find Jesus too—not in the familiar or safe but just beyond the edge of what I think I can handle.

*Because it's in those moments I suddenly find he's holding me.*

## Things Our Hearts Forget: You Don't Have to Hurry

We drive into Niagara-on-the-Lake. Just across from the falls and tourist attractions, it's a sleepy little town. I let out a sigh as I feel the rhythm and pace of this place. It is slower here.

Along the side of the road grows vineyard after vineyard. My husband and I point out different sizes of vines. "Those look young." "Those look like they've been growing a while."

We've read that vineyards can take years to produce. The green that flashes before us represents many seasons of patience, nurturing, faithfulness.

I'm not sure I could be a grape grower. I want things to work out now. I want to be better now. I want God's work to be complete in my life now.

And when that doesn't happen, *I feel like a failure.*

I remember something my wise friend Kristen Strong once said to me about the fruit of the Spirit. "Holley," she said, "it's fruit. It takes time to grow. We don't have those qualities all at once."

I smiled with relief.

Because while I may not ever be a grape grower, *I belong to one.*

He understands that we are in process. He doesn't mind the nurturing we need. He can see what's coming forth in our lives even when we feel like it will never happen.

We don't have to hurry our growth. In reality, our striving can no more produce fruit in our lives than a branch can instantly create a grape. In the end, we have to yield to greater timelines than our own.

So we wait. We trust. And when the time is right, we savor what God has done in us.

*What only he can do.*

## Things Our Hearts Forget: One Day You'll Be Home

The endless blue sky stretches above us. *"Let's sit on the patio for lunch,"* my husband says as we settle in at our favorite pizza place. I choose the seat looking outward, over the low fence and into the world. I can't see anyone but my husband next to me.

A few minutes later he leans in and whispers, "The table of women behind us is reading your book."

I slap his hand playfully and say, "No, they're not."

He repeats, "Really, they're reading your book." (This isn't the first time I've mistaken truth for teasing. I did the same thing when he proposed. But that's another story.)

I try to casually glance over my shoulder without looking like a stalker, and sure enough, about a dozen women have copies of my book in front of them. I can barely make out underlines and highlights on the pages. I hear laughter as well as heartfelt thoughts.

I turn back and sit still, stunned. Soon a grin spreads across my face and happy tears fill my eyes.

Because this is how we go through life, isn't it? We try to be obedient. We take our place at the table with Jesus. We love him.

But we don't always get to really see the results. We don't always know the impact.

And as I sat there, it seemed he whispered to my heart, "Heaven is when you get to turn the chair completely around."

Right now I type away at a keyboard a lot of the time. It's good and I'm so grateful. It's just that sometimes it's hard too. Sometimes it's lonely. Sometimes I wonder if it matters.

I imagine the same is true for you in whatever you're called to do—being a mama, struggling through a crisis, running a company, volunteering. You know what that thing is for you.

So I want to lean in and whisper to you, "Dear sister, trust that there is more than you can see. Trust that what you're doing makes a difference. Trust that one day you will get to turn the chair around and see fully."

"Now I know in part; then I shall know fully, even as I am fully known" (1 Cor. 13:12).

Until then, God gives us little glimpses, just like my husband did when he whispered a quiet word or two about what those women were doing that I couldn't see. We smiled together, the two of us. *And I think God smiles with us as we sit with him at the table of life too.*

Eventually our pizza was gone and it was the moment. Time to turn the chair around completely and see. And it was the most beautiful sight. Women of all ages and races. *The body of Christ.*

I fidgeted. I began to sweat. And just before they thought about calling security, I finally stammered out an awkward, "Um, hey, I wrote that book." Then before I knew it I had hugs thrown around my neck.

It felt like a welcome home.

And I tasted for a moment what it would be like to really be Home. *Sweet joy.*

Seeing the unseen. Knowing and touching and feeling what it means to be a small part of the very big work God is doing in the world.

You may not be able to see the difference you're making, the lives you're touching, the joy you're bringing. But it's there. It's real. It's truer than true. So sit at that table with Jesus. Do what he says. Give him your life and hold nothing back. Let him give you glimpses of glory.

Then one day he'll whisper the words, "It's time to turn the chair around, daughter." And you'll see, really see.

Then together we'll rejoice fully in what he's done.

Forever.

## Hold These Words Tight

What other words does your heart wonder about in the middle of the night, the quiet moments, the carpool line?

What are you afraid to believe but really, really wish you could?

*I'm loved.*

*I really can do this.*

*I'm chosen for a purpose.*

Whatever it is, it's scandalously true.

Not because you dreamed it up. Or you think it would be nice. Or maybe you've finally earned it.

It's true because the God who spoke the world into being has whispered his heart to you too.

*For as high as the heavens are above the earth,*
    *so great is his love for those who fear him. (Ps. 103:11)*

*This is what the Lord says . . .*
    *"I have summoned you by name; you are mine."*
    *(Isa. 43:1)*

I can do all this through him who gives me strength.

(Phil. 4:13)

We don't just have to wish. We can deep-in-our-bones know. Easy? Nope, not in this fallen world. But with the One who loves us and each other, it really is possible.

Sometimes what we need is even closer than we know—as close as the sunglasses we've been looking for that are already perched on our heads.

We can choose to always remember what our hearts never want to forget.

# 8

# You **Can** Make the Most of Change

A friend has a son going off to college in a few months. "It's going to be so different!" she declares.

A neighbor just found out her dad has been diagnosed with cancer and she'll need to help care for him. "This isn't what I expected in this season of my life," she shares.

A woman at church catches me up on the career transition she's making after being laid off. "I'm terrified and excited all at once!" she confesses.

It's been said that one of the only constants in our earthly lives is change. It's inevitable, it's continual, and it can be one of the greatest sources of stress for us. On the flip side, change is also where we have the most opportunity to grow and experience God in new ways.

I remember sitting in a class during graduate school as a professor drew a chart about change on the board. He listed major life events on it. Some were difficult, such as death or serious illness. Others were what we would label as happy, such as getting married or welcoming a new baby. What he said next totally changed my perspective. He shared that *both* types of events are stressful. In other words, they require lots of emotion and energy.

Remember what we talked about earlier in this book? We as humans crave homeostasis. We have internal thermostats that are always trying to get back to the same set point, the status quo. Any kind of change messes with that process. That's why you hear of so many newlyweds having a hard first year or new parents saying, "I didn't know it would be this hard." That's even truer when the change is unwelcome, such as a loss or significant unexpected shift.

God made us that way because otherwise the world would be in complete chaos. Think of the extreme change chasers you see on TV. They're always climbing the next mountain, marrying the next woman, trying the next drug. Even they have some kind of homeostatic mechanism within them. Imagine if they had none at all and if the rest of us didn't either. That's what it would take for us to love change all the time. So God knew what he was doing when he gave us that internal thermostat. He also made it so that change is an invitation to trust him. It is one of the biggest faith and intimacy builders we have.

And here's the good news: you know more about change than you realize. Even if you're the most change-resistant person ever, you have navigated through changes over and over again as you've lived. You learned to crawl, then walk, then run (although I choose *not* to run if I can help it). You've learned many other things too. You've seen God move. You've found out that other people can help you with the process of change.

When we're in the middle of change, it's usually so all-consuming that we don't stop to reflect on what's working well. We sometimes come up with strategies or find solutions without even realizing we're doing so. That's why we're going to take some time to slow down now. We'll talk through what change means as well as what we can continue to do to thrive in the midst of it.

## Defining Change

What *is* change? We can list examples of it such as a move, having a baby, or losing a loved one. But actually putting definitive words to what change means can be far more difficult. When I paused to do so, I realized there are two major types of change: anticipated change and unanticipated change.

*Anticipated change*—In this type of change, we know about whatever is coming. We know our kids will go off to college one day. We know we will have to move to another state because of a job change. We know the chronic illness we have is progressive. What makes this type of change stressful is not that we don't know what's going to happen but rather that knowing and experiencing are two different things. Even when our minds can say, "Yes, this is going to happen," we can't fully prepare the rest of us for what it will be like. As the change actually unfolds, we learn to adjust.

*Unanticipated change*—In this type of change, we didn't see what was coming, or we didn't picture it accurately. We get married to the "perfect" spouse and are blindsided by an affair twenty years later. We have property damage on our new house from a tornado. We get promoted to a position higher than we ever dreamed possible. In these scenarios, change means that what we expected and what actually happened don't match. We're caught off guard and need to make unplanned adjustments, sometimes very quickly. In most cases, this type of change is more stressful because it's an instant interruption rather than a gradual one.

In both types of change, what's required of us is a response. Perhaps that's one of the reasons change is so stressful—it forces us to decide to *do something* (and yes, even ignoring the change and pretending nothing happened is still a decision). Any time we have to take action, we must use our internal resources. It requires energy and emotion. Change always costs us. There's simply no way around it. But here's the encouraging part: we can move through change and say either, "What a waste" or "That was so worth it."

## Go Ahead, Be a Control Freak

After you finish making a copy of the phrase above and showing it to your husband or posting it on your cubicle wall, let's talk about what I really mean.

All the way back in the first chapter of Genesis, God spoke to man for the very first time. "God blessed them and said to them, 'Be fruitful and increase in number; fill the earth and subdue it'" (Gen. 1:28). Even before the fall, God's plan was for man to take responsibility for his life and what was under his stewardship.

Research has shown that we feel significant stress when we are completely out of control. Author John Ortberg shares this insight:

> In concentration camps or prisoner of war environments, the greatest difference between people who give up and people who remain resilient is a sense that they can still control something, according to psychologist Julius Segal. In nursing homes, such trivial choices as getting to decide when to see a movie or how to arrange their rooms made seniors' health and emotional well-being improve and the death rate drop.[1]

Stripped of every other opportunity to control, some concentration camp survivors said they simply chose their attitudes. It was the one thing no one could take away from them. Even that seemingly small decision made a significant difference.

When I'm stressed, I clean the house. Now, I'm not Martha Stewart, and I've encountered dust bunnies that could pass for small dinosaurs in age as well as in size. But if the rest of my life feels out of control, I need to do something. I've heard other women say the same.

We often feel guilty about this tendency within ourselves. People in our lives may even say, "Why can't you just let it go?" But that desire to control is a very natural and essential part of who we're created to be.

Now here's the catch: the kind of control we're made for isn't *ultimate* control—it's *secondary* control.

> What causes fights and quarrels among you? Don't they come from your desires that battle within you? You desire but do not have, so you kill. You covet but you cannot get what you want, so you quarrel and fight. You do not have because you do not ask God. When you ask, you do not receive, because you ask with wrong motives, that you may spend what you get on your pleasures. . . . Submit yourselves, then, to God. Resist the devil, and he will flee from you. (James 4:1–3, 7)

In other words, the self-control we're asked to exercise in our lives comes out of a complete submission to God first. We release everything in our lives to him. Then he gives much of it back to us to steward and care for as his servants.

When it comes to control, the key is motivation. Are we trying to get what we want or force something to happen? Or are we living in biblical stewardship in which we say, "God, everything

I have and all that I am is yours. Your kingdom come and your will be done in my life. Now show me how to take responsibility for my life and to respond in a way that honors you"?

This matters first because it's what God has asked of us. But it's also the only way to keep from driving ourselves nuts in a world that is constantly changing. Demanding our way is very different from proactively responding through the Spirit. When we try to have ultimate control, we become exhausted, frustrated, and bitter. If you need an example of this, just go find a two-year-old.

Our experience of change is transformed when we realize we are not the final decision maker. So we do what we can and then yield as Jesus did in the Garden of Gethsemane: "Not my will, but yours be done" (Luke 22:42). Ironically, the most powerful freedom turns out to be surrender.

## Taking Charge of Change

Sometimes people respond to what I shared above by saying, "After I've surrendered to God's will, then I'm supposed to sit back and see what happens." But that's not the pattern we find in Scripture, except in some cases in which people are specifically told to wait. More often, taking action follows submitting to God.

Change is disorienting because it feels like it happens *to* us. We then feel out of control, and that can lead to negative emotions as well as poor choices. So the next step when dealing with change is to come up with a plan of action.

We like to skip this part. At least I do. I'd rather whine, take a nap, and eat chocolate when change comes into my life. I don't want to sit down and prayerfully consider how to respond to what has happened to me. Aren't I the victim? Don't I deserve to throw a nice little pity party? Just talking about making a plan makes me want to stick out my tongue at these words. Feel free to join me.

But proactively addressing change is actually the best way to thrive in the midst of it. Ortberg describes that approach this way: "Part of what God made you for [is] to be a powerful and creative force for good in the world. When our sense of dominion dies—when we feel like we have no control over our lives—then we die as well."[2] Perhaps *die* seems like a strong word, but I believe it's accurate. We may not lose our lives physically, but we'll lose ourselves in other significant ways.

Look at the world around you: growth and change are the hallmarks of life. The only things in this world that are not growing or changing are not alive.

When you refuse to change, you begin to die in some small way.

But that doesn't have to happen, because the reverse is also true. When you embrace change, you begin to live and grow in some small way—and often in very big ways.

This can begin with deciding to simply say, "I am not a victim. I'm a child of God who still has a choice."

## Knowing What's under Your Control

We tend to resist change, but there's one area in which we're quite enthusiastic about it. I've seen it again and again in counseling sessions. We're talking through a difficult issue and my client seems quite down. Then when I ask her what she would like to change, her face suddenly lights up. "My husband, kids, dog, and in-laws. Then the neighbors, the grouchy woman at church, and that mean girl from high school . . ." Okay, maybe the list isn't quite that extensive. But there's no getting around this: we love the idea of changing other people! I do too. I'd love to have a magic wand to carry around with me so I could turn inconsiderate people into kind ones. Or at least whack them on the head with it.

But I digress. The point is that other people are not on our "what we can change" list. Doing so violates free will, and as we all know, that's a principle God is very passionate about keeping intact.

One of my favorite books of all time is *Boundaries: When to Say Yes, When to Say No to Take Control of Your Life*. Authors Dr. Henry Cloud and Dr. John Townsend describe our lives as a lot like our yards. They say:

> Knowing what I am to own and take responsibility for gives me freedom. If I know where my yard begins and ends, I am free to do with it what I like. Taking responsibility for my life opens up many different options. However, if I do not "own" my life, my choices and options become very limited.[3]

Cloud and Townsend go on to share a list of what God has placed within our yards. In other words, what we are to "have dominion over" in our lives.

### What's within Our Boundaries?

- Feelings
- Attitudes and beliefs
- Behaviors
- Choices
- Values
- Limits
- Talents
- Thoughts
- Desires
- Love[4]

In other words, we can control what's inside us. We can't control other people, many of the circumstances of our lives, some aspects of our health, and a lot of the other things that we wish we could. We don't like this reality. But accepting it is, ironically, the first step toward true freedom. We need our energy and emotion so we can focus on the list above. If we're fixated on what "isn't in our yards," then we're going to be exhausted and frustrated.

*What else do you wish was on the list above? How can you release it to God?*

---
 

---
 

---

We may think, "If I can't control what I really want to, then why does this list above even matter?" What God has put "under your dominion" matters because while you can't use these things to control, you can use them to *influence*.

You can't force people to change, but you can love them well and pray for them.

You can't avoid all health challenges, but you can eat well and exercise to prevent many of them.

You can't make the door to your dream job open, but you can make the most of your strengths, gifts, and opportunities so you're prepared for what God has for you.

We talked earlier about how even those who found themselves in concentration camps benefited from taking charge of what they could. Perhaps the most famous of these is Viktor Frankl, a psychiatrist from Vienna. He lost his freedom, family members, home, and much more. But in the midst of the darkest circumstances many of us can imagine, this idea helped him persevere: "Everything can be taken from a man but one thing: the last of the human freedoms—to choose one's attitude in any given set of circumstances, to choose one's own way."[5]

Viktor Frankl knew what was in his yard. His body may have been in a concentration camp, but the rest of him remained free. He took changes that seemed impossible to handle and transformed them into opportunities.

You always have a choice. It's a God-given gift that can never, ever be taken away even by the worst circumstances or the greatest evil.

## What Will You Do about Changes in Your Life?

At this point, you have come to a crossroads, my friend. You know what's in your yard and what's not. Now you get to decide what to do about it. Our choices are always multidimensional. They involve all of us as complete people: spiritual, emotional, social, and physical. When we think of how we want to adapt to change, all of those aspects are important to consider. Let's talk through some questions that will help you make a plan when you face change.

### What Does God Want Me to Do?

As we talked about before, we have secondary control, but God still ultimately decides. So seeking his will is always the first step. This happens in several ways.

*His Word*—What does Scripture say that applies to your situation? A helpful tool for finding out can be sites such as Crosswalk .com or BibleGateway.com. They have online versions of the Bible that you can search by keyword. For example, if you're struggling with a difficult person in your life, you can go online and search for the word *love* in the New Testament. Then you can copy what stands out most to you and paste it into a document to reread and study further.

*The Holy Spirit*—Jesus promised the Holy Spirit would "guide you into all the truth" (John 16:13), so sometimes the direction we're supposed to go isn't written out in black and white. Sometimes it's a leading we sense from deep down inside. Ask the Holy Spirit to show you what you need to do. Then test what you hear against Scripture and talk about it with godly people.

*Trusted people*—We are made for community, and God uses other believers to help us on our journey. Ask those in your life who listen to him and love you for their insights and advice. "For lack of guidance a nation falls, but victory is won through many advisers" (Prov. 11:14).

After you've sought wisdom in these ways, *do something*. The worst decision is no decision at all. If you truly feel that you are to wait, set an amount of time to do so and then reevaluate. Even the Scripture that we like to quote most about waiting—"Be still, and know that I am God" (Ps. 46:10)—involves two proactive phrases: *be still* and *know*.

What I've more often seen (and done) is making the lack of specific instructions from God that I'd like to have (for example, an email from him) a reason not to do anything at all. I finally found a lot of comfort in this verse: "Many are the plans in a person's heart, but it is the LORD's purpose that prevails" (Prov. 19:21). In other words, we are supposed to plan. We are supposed to move forward. And if we happen to go the wrong direction, God is able to redirect us and still get us to his purposes in the end.

You are not made for passivity and inaction. Either proactively decide to wait, or take the next step.

## What's the Best Use of My Emotions and Energy?

After you decide on your next step, you can strategize so that you move forward in the most effective, efficient way. I grew up in

Texas with blistering summers and scorching heat. I remember trying to fry an egg on the driveway on one particularly ambitious day. One of the refrains my brother and I heard often was, "Shut the door behind you, please." We gladly complied because we understood air-conditioning was a valuable commodity. If we wanted to flop on the couch in comfort after playing outside, we had to make sure the temperature stayed down.

In much the same way, taking a step toward change can open the doors on our energy and emotions. We find ourselves spilling those valuable resources all over the place. We quickly become exhausted from the heat of what we're facing and then feel as if there's no refuge because what we need seems to have escaped.

A season of change is like summer—it's a time for making sure the doors are shut and the windows are closed. In other words, what we might be able to get by with on a beautiful, peaceful fall day is not going to cut it now.

If it feels like you are leaking energy and emotions, then it's time to do an inventory.

*What are the commitments in your life right now that take emotion and energy?* (Marriage, kids, taking care of the house, dealing with doctors' appointments, searching for work, etc.)

.......................................................................................................................

.......................................................................................................................

.......................................................................................................................

.......................................................................................................................

*Now review the list and circle any that are not optional. If they are not optional, are there ways you can get help with any of them? Write those below. (Right now just let yourself dream.*

For example, getting a maid might not seem possible, but write it down anyway.)

_____

_____

*Write down any commitments that are optional right now. In other words, you could say no or later to them.*

_____

_____

_____

Did you feel frustrated when you were writing those lists? If so, that's totally normal. You may have even thought, "But, Holley, you don't understand the reality I'm dealing with right now." And you're absolutely right. I don't understand. Only you do. That's why you're the one filling in those blanks. No one else knows your life like you do. You can do whatever you want with what you wrote above—ignore it, implement it, burn it in the backyard.

The point I'm trying to make is that *you have permission* to be strategic about your life, especially in times of change.

We like to pretend we're superwomen. We go through life checking off our endless to-do lists. Then change comes and we keep right on going. We begin to feel more frustrated and weary, so we berate ourselves and feel guilty. We say, "I should be able to handle this!"

But we're not superwomen (and who wants to wear tights all the time anyway?). We're human and we have limits. This is not a sign of weakness; it's a gift.

Let's use another analogy that I love. It's like we have internal emotional and energy bank accounts. We've budgeted well and can cover all our expenses. Then someone runs the family car into a pole, and suddenly we need to buy a new vehicle. So what do we do? For the next few months, we change our spending.

That's also what we do when we face change. We temporarily alter how we spend our emotions and energy. This can be difficult because often the many things we do are part of our self-worth. That means when we slow down or switch things up, we feel like a failure. But the opposite is true. Sustainable life success is only possible when we can adjust in times of change to avoid going into life overdraft.

It can also be hard to explain to people why we're making adjustments. If that's true of you, here's one way you can say it:

"I'm going through some changes in my life right now (if this is a safe person, share a little bit about what's happening—but you don't have to). I've learned that our emotions and energy are like internal bank accounts. Right now it feels like I've got some extra bills coming in! So for (period of time—days, weeks, months, this year) I need to adjust. Even though I love (whatever it is you're doing that you'll need to cut back on or stop), I've had to make a really hard choice about it. Here's what I've decided to do: (If you can, offer a timeline or alternative, such as 'I will not be on the committee this fall, but I would love to check in with you next spring after things have settled down again'). I value our relationship, and that has been one of the most difficult parts of this for me. Are we still okay? Will you support me in this?"

In my experience, people are most often understanding and gracious. If they're not, then realize it most likely has nothing to do with you. Remember how we talked about controlling what's in your yard? They have a yard too—and you're not in it. They may express emotions like, "I'm disappointed or sad." That's totally appropriate, and you can affirm that emotion without changing your decision. Ask yourself, "How is this going to impact them?" and then try to offer a solution or at least reassure them (for example, "I'm really going to miss being there because X means a lot to me and so do you").

Warning: this will be hard. Your heart will feel like it's going to pound out of your chest. But you will survive, I promise. And in the middle of change, you will be one of the few people who are still able to thrive because you have the resources you need. That will ultimately benefit not only you but everyone in your life too.

## What Do I Need Most Right Now?

After you've set boundaries, it's time to figure out what you really need in this time of transition. A little gardening taught me a lot in this area.

I have a black thumb when it comes to plants. I walk through the garden center and you can almost hear the little sprouts saying, "Don't pick me! Don't pick me!" I've recently decided to try to break my "kill the plants" streak. So on my last trip to the store I scooped up a tomato plant.

When I brought it home, my husband asked me a bunch of questions: How much water does it need? What kind of light does it like best? When does it produce tomatoes?

I had the same brilliant answer for each one: "I don't know." And thus began my education on why my plants don't often survive.

We can treat the "yard" of our lives in much the same way. We have high hopes for what we will be and what we can do. Then we wonder why the grass keeps turning brown. We're so busy that we forget to pause and ask the basic questions about what we really need.

That's never truer than in times of stress and change. You are going to require extra TLC. Here's the deal: it's your yard. And the way you grow and thrive is different from anyone else, so it's up to you to know what you need. No one else can do it for you.

............

We practiced naming our needs earlier in this book, but I believe it's important enough to revisit. Pause for a moment and consider:

*When are the moments I feel most joy? What am I doing?* The answer can be as simple as talking with a friend or baking cookies. When change hits us, our moments of joy are most often the first to go. But you need those more than ever. Make time in your schedule for them.

We'll talk more about this in the coming chapters, but for now know that what brings you joy is most likely tied to your strengths, your gifts, and the purpose God has for your life. What might seem like something insignificant can turn out to be very meaningful.

*When do I feel closest to God?* I love the book *Sacred Pathways* by Gary Thomas because he explains that although we all connect with God in certain ways like reading the Bible, our spiritual lives are unique and we have different avenues of feeling close to him. For example, I feel closest to God when I learn something new about him or encounter him through other people. My husband feels closest to God when he sees God's glory in nature or is doing something physical like riding his bike.

When you are in a time of change, people will throw all kinds of spiritual advice at you. They will tell you to get up at 5:00 a.m. to pray for an hour. Or go on a silent retreat. Or make ten new best friends. What they are telling you is this: *what has worked well for them.* If it turns out to be true for you too, great. If not, you are allowed to do something else. Whatever it is, just make time to do it.

*What are the hardest moments for me and what helps?* Just like we need to be familiar with our joys, we also need to be acquainted with our sorrows. What hurts most about the change you're going through will be different for you than for most other people. Identify your low points, and then also consider what might help you get through them. For example, if your chemo appointments are the hardest for you, you might need to bring along the friend who makes you laugh the loudest.

You don't have to "grin and bear it." You don't have to trudge through and pretend like you're really doing okay. It's totally fine to say, "You know what, I hate this part. I need help with it." That's not a sign of weakness but a sign of strength. People want to share what you're going through but may not know how. When you tell them what they can do to help, you give them a beautiful gift.

*What standards am I holding myself to that I need to let go of?* When we are in the middle of significant change, we've entered "special circumstances." In other words, the regular rules no longer apply. Because we have that inner drive to keep the status quo, we often fight with all our might to keep what we consider our "normal." And that's fine up to a point. But when we begin to exhaust ourselves, it's time to come up with a different strategy. There's no shame in saying, "Right now I need to do things differently." It doesn't mean you've failed. It doesn't mean you've given up. It doesn't mean you won't ever get back to "normal." It just means you're being wise with the decisions you're making.

Your yard is constantly growing and changing. Sometimes it needs more water. Other times it needs less. When you give it what it needs, you're simply being a good steward.

*Look through your answers to all of the above. What's one way you'll respond to the changes in your life?*

-------------------------------------------------------------

-------------------------------------------------------------

When you start to feel exhausted and out of control, go through this process again. Change isn't a single event; it's a process. And checking on how you're doing can help you keep adjusting. See how your yard is doing.

# Why You Can Handle Change

Here's the sneaky thing about change: we don't even realize when we've adapted to it. You've experienced lots of change in your life.

You went from living in a womb to making your way in this crazy world.

You used to crawl and now you walk.

You probably grew up in one house and now live in a different one.

You switched grades every single year and survived.

You may have gone from single to married, then from being just a couple to having kids.

You have experienced winter, spring, summer, and fall numerous times.

And along the way, you have most likely made your way through some other significant changes as well.

If you are alive and breathing right now, you know how to survive change. The thing is, when we've adjusted to change, we stop calling it "change" and just call it "normal." The changes of yesterday make up the normal of today.

That's a gift, but it can also make us more afraid of change than is really needed. Every time we confront change, it feels like the first time. And it is, for that particular one. But the pattern of change is built into who we are as people. We are made to grow. We are made to overcome obstacles. We are made to keep moving forward until we're home with Jesus.

Yes, some changes are far more welcome than others.

But none of them is too difficult for God.

And because he lives within you, none of them is too difficult for you either.

You don't have to like change.

Some changes you'll even hate.

And that's totally okay.

What we're talking about here is what you'll do with the inevitable. It may seem as if all other choices have been stripped away, but your ability to choose how you respond to your circumstances can never be.

Sometimes change will even turn out to be a gift in surprise packaging. The move you didn't want to make may lead you to some of your dearest friends. That cancer you didn't want to fight may carve out a well of compassion within you that refreshes others. That job you didn't want to lose may open the door to an opportunity you never could have taken otherwise.

You have what it takes to thrive through change, my friend.

Dare to open your arms and heart to what life brings.

And know that for the parts that are painful, someone else has opened his arms to take the worst of that blow for you. Jesus stretched out on a cross in the ultimate acceptance of change so that he could walk with you and give you life in the middle of everything that comes your way.

He understands change is hard. He understands you may not want it. He understands you may wish your circumstances were different.

He knows.

And he knows you.

He knows who you are now and who you are becoming—and he's committed to redeeming the changes, all of them, so that nothing is ever wasted in the yard of your life. Even compost can serve a purpose.

The grass isn't greener on the other side after all.

It's greenest where you help it grow.

# 9

# Your Future
# Is Full of **Hope**

The headlines scroll across the bottom of the screen with quiet
intensity.

Economic downturn anticipated.

Severe storms heading north.

Study shows plastic may cause cancer.

On and on the list goes with words for every area of our
lives. The one element they have in common? An attempt to
make the future more predictable. Even if what we hear strikes
fear within us, at least we feel like we have more control over
what's coming.

But the reality is that we don't know the future.

We can't predict what's really ahead.

And most of all, we certainly can't control it.

If your stomach tightened a little bit as you read those sentences, that simply means you're human. We are wired to be vigilant. Our brains look for possible threats so we can avoid them. That's a helpful feature of our minds that makes life much easier to navigate.

But sometimes, especially when we're experiencing stress, that ability goes into overdrive. We become hypervigilant and spend a lot of time thinking about things that are never likely to happen or that we can't prevent even if they are going to take place.

Another name for that tendency? Worry.

I don't want to make y'all jealous or anything, but I have some serious worrying skills. I can gnaw on one thought like my little beagle-basset chews on a bone. I can carry it with me for days. Sometimes I bury it and then dig it up again. If anyone dares to mess with it, I might even growl.

Can you relate?

The good news is that if you can, then you already have the skills you need to change how you think about the future. *Worry transformed turns into hope and faith.* We can replace all those negative, fearful thoughts with truthful, positive ones. You've built up those chew-on-a-thought muscles in your mind all these years. Now it's time to put them to better use.

## Rediscovering Hope

The way our minds work becomes evident as I sit in an audience with hundreds of women. The keynote speaker, Brené Brown, is setting up a scenario for us: A family is driving down the highway on the way to Grandma's house. The sun is shining, the birds are singing, everyone is laughing, and then . . .

She asks us what happens next. "Did any of you picture a car accident or something else bad happening?" Hands shoot up around the room as we nervously smile and confess our thoughts.

Brené goes on to explain this as the vigilance I described earlier. Then she essentially says something that I'll never forget: "Joy is the most vulnerable emotion."[1]

I'm stunned. In our culture, joy is often brushed off as easy or even shallow. But I dig deeper. I look at studies. I read more from Brené, who is a researcher as well as an author.

Again and again I find the same thing: our natural outlook on the future is fear. Perhaps that's why God says to his people over and over again, "Do not be afraid." I love that he uses "be" so often. To me it says he knows we're tempted to be afraid, but he's just asking us not to stay that way. He has a better plan for us instead.

So what replaces worries and fears about the future? Hope and faith.

Neither one of them is an easy word. No matter how many years of Sunday school we've attended, how often we've watched God move in our lives, how intellectually certain we are of what we believe, choosing hope and faith over worry and fear is something we'll have to do again and again.

The first step is to stop feeling guilty that we're not some wonder-Christian who can look at the future with bright, shiny eyes and declare that all will be well. There's no such person on this planet. And if someone tries to tell you it's always like that for them, then their method of dealing with worry and fear is most likely denial. I'm just sayin'.

So let's agree that we're all in this together and that God is on our side because he understands how challenging this is for us. Yet he still invites us to live and think in a beautifully different way.

# The Future Is Out of Our Hands

Let's think back for a moment to when we talked about what's in the "yard" of our lives. In other words, what God asks us to have dominion over.

*The future is not on that list.*

Never has been, never will be.

Oh, we want it to be. We'd love a genie in a bottle that will make our wishes come true. Or a time travel machine so we can see next week or next year. We'd love a fast-forward button on the remote control of life.

But it just doesn't work that way. So we worry.

*Worry is an attempt to control what we can never control.* That's why it's so hard to stop. It's like putting our minds on a treadmill and saying, "When I reach the end of the block, then I'll get off." But the trouble is, we never really go anywhere.

Worry is an illusion. It's a master trickster that tells us, "If you are just vigilant enough, if you are just cautious enough, then bad things won't happen." We use it like a form of protection around our lives and the lives of those we love. But it doesn't really exist. That wall we think we're building is made of paper.

> Therefore I tell you, do not worry about your life, what you will eat or drink; or about your body, what you will wear. Is not life more than food, and the body more than clothes? Look at the birds of the air; they do not sow or reap or store away in barns, and yet your heavenly Father feeds them. Are you not much more valuable than they? Can any one of you by worrying add a single hour to your life?
>
> And why do you worry about clothes? See how the flowers of the field grow. They do not labor or spin. Yet I tell you that not even Solomon in all his splendor was

dressed like one of these. If that is how God clothes the grass of the field, which is here today and tomorrow is thrown into the fire, will he not much more clothe you—you of little faith? So do not worry, saying, "What shall we eat?" or "What shall we drink?" or "What shall we wear?" For the pagans run after all these things, and your heavenly Father knows that you need them. But seek first his kingdom and his righteousness, and all these things will be given to you as well. Therefore do not worry about tomorrow, for tomorrow will worry about itself. Each day has enough trouble of its own. (Matt. 6:25-34)

It turns out worry has been around since the time of Jesus (and even longer). The phrase he uses to describe us worriers is interesting: "you of little faith" (Matt. 6:30). Yet in another verse he says that if we have faith "as small as a mustard seed," then we can move mountains (Matt. 17:20). Have you seen a mustard seed? It's tiny. So it's okay to have little faith—what matters is where we're placing whatever faith we do have. Worriers place their faith in their ability to "control" the future. Jesus asks us to place our faith firmly in him instead.

## How Do We Stop Worrying and Start Believing?

When I think about moving from worry to faith, my first inner response is, "I can't do that." But as we talked about before, if you know how to worry, then you know how to have hope and faith. It's the same thought pattern with a different focus.

What makes it difficult is that we always feel fear when we make that switch. We experience a lack of control (which is not real—because we don't control the future anyway). Our minds fight to reclaim our patterns of worry because they like to maintain the status quo.

So switching to living in hope and faith never happens automatically. It also never happens just by deciding to do so. Saying, "I'm going to stop worrying and start believing" is a little like saying, "I'm going to stop living here and start living in Hawaii" without ever catching a plane.

Moving from fear and worry to faith and hope is *a process*. Of course, we intellectually know it's what we should do. But we still have to do the hard work of making it happen. Essentially, we need to be "transformed by the renewing of your mind" (Rom. 12:2).

As we discussed earlier, our thoughts create literal neural pathways in our minds. That means the ways we habitually think become the mental roads of least resistance. Your brain is efficient. So when you need to instantly decide how to react to something, it always picks the most well-worn path. If you've worried a lot like I have, then your brain is automatically going to pick worry as its first choice when it comes to thinking about the future.

What we're doing is deciding to let the grass grow over that pathway and create a new one instead. Just like it would in the physical world, this takes time and effort. But with the help of the Holy Spirit, it is possible.

Let's start with some small steps in a new direction.

## Recognize Worry and Fear

Because worrying comes so naturally to us, we often don't even realize we're doing it. So the first step is to simply start noticing when negative thoughts about the future creep into your mind.

One of the odd little quirks about our minds is that worry often ambushes us when things are good. We're having dinner with friends, laughing and talking, all feels right with the world, and suddenly we think, "What if the house is burning down right now?" It seems like such an out-of-nowhere thought that we wonder if it might actually be true. Have you ever had that happen?

That is your brain being a guard dog. Remember how part of its job is to detect threats? Well, that means if there aren't any, then it tends to think it must be missing something. So it comes up with a possible threat. If that happens to you, just act like your brain is being a good guard dog, pat it on the head, and say, "Thank you, but that burglar you think you see is just a sheet on a clothesline. Everything is okay." Then whisper a prayer like this: "God, thank you that you are in control, you know everything, and you have promised to take care of me."

## Replace Worry and Fear with a Different Thought

Right now I want you to close your eyes and stop thinking. Don't think about your day. Don't think about your family. Don't think about the dog.

Did it work?

Nope.

Our minds can't *not* think. That means you will always have a thought in your mind at any given moment.

So recognizing worry is only the beginning; we have to replace those thoughts with something else.

As a starting point, it helps to come up with the complete opposite scenario of the worry. So if you suddenly think, "The house is burning down," then ask yourself, "What else could be true?" For example, someone could be ringing your doorbell to tell you that you've won a million dollars.

Does that sound ridiculous? Well, so is thinking the house is burning down. Your mind just takes that thought more seriously because it labels it as a threat.

What you're showing your mind by thinking the opposite way is that it's most likely not being rational. It's also one of the quickest ways to get your mind off that well-worn worry path and to start putting a new one in place.

Of course, the above is just an exercise to get you started. What we really want to replace worry with is *truth*.

Jesus said, "You will know the truth, and the truth will set you free" (John 8:32). Jesus also said, "I am the way and the truth and the life" (John 14:6). When he invites us to know the truth, it's not an intellectual invitation. (In fact, you may have noticed that if you just try to tell your mind a "true" cliché, it only panics more. That's because you're speaking to only your neocortex, the logical part of you. But the limbic system and brain stem aren't buying it, so they keep on sounding the alarm.) What Jesus is extending here is an invitation to know *him*. This isn't simply intellectual truth. It's *relational* and *emotional* truth too. It asks us to place our trust not in what we know but in who we know.

## Learn to Trust

Faith and hope have the same foundation—trust. And trust comes from knowing someone's character. Perhaps even more so, it comes from knowing they care about you.

*Worry and fear come from believing a lie about who God is.*

I didn't want to write that sentence. I hovered over the delete button. I stretched my arms and thought about going to get a cookie. But there's just not any way around it.

That being said, let me also say we all struggle with worry at some point. Every single one of us. It doesn't mean that God is mad at you or you're a failure. It simply means it's time to make some changes.

And we don't have to make those changes on our own. Jesus said the job of the Holy Spirit is to "guide you into all truth" (see

John 16:13). I love the word *guide* because it's an ongoing process rather than a one-time occurrence. As long as we are in this fallen world, we will uncover lies and the Holy Spirit will help us replace them with truth.

I also want to clarify that not worrying doesn't mean we don't think about the future or that we aren't concerned.

We are to *wonder* about the future. That means considering what may be ahead so we can plan wisely.

We are also to love one another, and that means we will feel *concern* for our brothers and sisters. The difference is that concern ultimately releases people to God, while worry places the burdens of their lives on our shoulders.

If you're not sure whether what you're doing is worry or wonder and concern, then pause and ask this: "Am I thinking from a place of fear or a place of faith?" Most of the time, the answer will be fear. That's okay as a starting point. Then just simply be honest with God. "Lord, I feel fear, but I know you don't want me to stay afraid. Please help me change my thoughts." Our part is fighting that fear and consistently choosing to focus on what God says instead.

In order to be able to fight fear, we need to have plenty of ammunition. That means knowing who God is and what he has promised.

## What's True of Your Future No Matter What

If God had a news ticker like the one on our TV screens, certain messages would be sent to our hearts again and again.

*God is with you*—"Never will I leave you; never will I forsake you" (Heb. 13:5). When stress and hard times come, God can feel distant. We wonder where he went or if perhaps we've done something wrong. But God has promised that he will always be with us. It's okay to ask him to remind you of his love. "God, I know you're with me. I believe you when you say that you will never leave me. I feel weak right now. Can you please help me see one way you're with me today?"

*God is for you*—"If God is for us, who can be against us?" (Rom. 8:31). One of the biggest lies the enemy will try to tell you is that God is not for you. We know our imperfections and weaknesses, so it's easy for the enemy to slip in and say, "You must have really blown it. Look how God is punishing you."

But the truth is, we have been rescued from God's punishment through Christ. "This is what your Sovereign LORD says, your God, who defends his people: 'See, I have taken out of your hand the cup that made you stagger; from that cup, the goblet of my wrath, you will never drink again'" (Isa. 51:22). In the Garden of Gethsemane, Jesus prayed for this "cup" to pass from him if possible. Yet ultimately he surrendered to God's will and took the wrath we deserve. Yes, at times God disciplines us as his children for our good. But because of what Christ did, we will never face his wrath. God is for us.

*God is in control*—"When I consider your heavens, the work of your fingers, the moon and the stars, which you have set in place, what is mankind that you are mindful of them, human beings that you care for them?" (Ps. 8:3–4). We are not in control. We are not out of control either. We are *in God's control.*

Yes, things happen this side of heaven that we just can't understand. We may want a different outcome. Yet at some point we must decide if we will be ruler of our lives or if we will let God take his rightful place. We are not made for control, and as long as we strive after it, we'll be disappointed and exhausted.

*God makes you victorious*—"In all these things we are more than conquerors through him who loved us" (Rom. 8:37). Paul has just listed some of the most difficult things we can face in this life. We hope what he's going to say next is, "But because you now belong to Jesus, none of this will happen to you. You and those you love will always be safe." But he doesn't make any promises about our circumstances; instead, he reassures us of who we are. We will have hard things happen in our lives. We will face loss. We will be under stress at times. But God does promise that *who we are* is not changed by any of this. We will be victorious no matter what.

*God provides for you*—"My God will meet all your needs according to the riches of his glory in Christ Jesus" (Phil. 4:19). I'd like to stop this verse just after the first few words, "My God will meet all your needs." I have strong opinions about my needs. For example, a chocolate cookie with no calories. But that one little phrase in the verse changes everything: "*according to his.*" That means God meets our needs as he sees best and in line with his purposes. That means we don't always get what we want. God alone knows our hearts, and he does promise we will always have what we need.

*God has a good plan for you*—"'For I know the plans I have for you,' declares the LORD, 'plans to prosper you and not to harm you, plans to give you hope and a future'" (Jer. 29:11). We love to quote this verse perhaps more than any other in Scripture. We hold it up like a shield guaranteeing that nothing bad will happen to us. In my life, I did so during the more than seven years my husband and I struggled with infertility. After a while, I started whining to God about Jeremiah 29:11. One day it seemed his Spirit gently whispered in response, "Holley, I had good plans for my Son too, but they still included a cross." We don't escape heartache and trouble in this life. But we do have the promise that this isn't the end of the story. God is working out his plan and nothing can stop him.

*God is not holding out on you*—"He who did not spare his own Son, but gave him up for us all—how will he not also, along with him, graciously give us all things?" (Rom. 8:32). When our dreams

You're Going to Be Okay

don't come true in the ways we imagined, it's easy to assume God is somehow depriving us. But if that were true, he never would have sent Jesus.

God has already given you what is most precious to him, and that means there is nothing he's not willing to give you. Does that mean we always get what we want? Nope. But we can trust that when we don't, there are greater purposes at work, and it's not because God is holding out on us.

*God is always the same*—"Jesus Christ is the same yesterday and today and forever" (Heb. 13:8). In all of the above, what matters most is that our future is secure not in circumstances but in a Person.

A God who loves you.

A God who holds the world in his hands.

A God who gave his Son for you.

A God who does not change.

Yes, how God works is always changing in remarkably creative ways. But his character is firm forever. That means what's most certain about your future is *God himself.* When nothing makes sense, when all your expectations fall short, when your plans get derailed, there is only One who can offer you a firm foundation for whatever is ahead. When you place your life in God's hands, your future is secure.

Think of a challenging situation in your life right now, and then walk through these questions.

*Who is God showing himself to be in this situation? What is he revealing to you about his character?*

178

*What else do you need to know about him right now? Ask him to show you.*

_____

_____

*How is who he is showing you more about who you are? (For example, "Because God is always with me, I am never alone.")*

_____

_____

*How do you want to become more like him through this situation?*

_____

_____

_____

. . . . . . . . . . . . . . . . . . . . . . . . . . . . . . . . . . . . . . . . . .

We all must build the foundation of our future somewhere.

> Therefore everyone who hears these words of mine and puts them into practice is like a wise man who built his house on the rock. The rain came down, the streams rose, and the winds blew and beat against that house; yet it did not fall, because it had its foundation on the rock. (Matt. 7:24–25)

Jesus *is* the rock. The words he tells us to put into practice aren't just about how we are to live but are about who he is and who we are in him.

Life's storms will come, but the One who calmed the wind and waves can make sure that when the rain ends, you are still standing strong in faith and hope, secure in his arms.

## Creative Ways to Retrain Your Brain

Once we set our minds on truth, the next step is to teach our thoughts to stay there. For example, as you read about who God is above, you probably nodded in agreement. And yet the next time someone cuts you off in traffic, all of that just may go flying out the window along with one of your fingers. Ahem.

Knowing the truth is the first part. Applying it is the second.

That takes us back to how our brains are wired and what we need to do to "transform" them. So let's talk through some practical ways to retrain your brain.

The key is repetition, repetition, repetition. At some point, new thoughts become automatic. But at the beginning, transforming your mind requires being very intentional.

### Keep God's Word in Front of You

Jesus said that we don't live on bread alone but on every word that comes from the mouth of the Lord (see Matt. 4:4). When I skip a meal, I get grouchy. And when our hearts don't get the spiritual food we need, the same thing tends to happen. I always wanted to be one of those women who got up at 5:00 a.m. and spent an hour reading the Bible. But I'm not. And I'm never going to be. I'm guessing you probably aren't either. *That's okay.* Just find a way to regularly get God's Word into your heart.

Here's how that has worked out for me. We have a stationary bike in the back room of our house. I ride it in the morning and check my email when I do. So I signed up with BibleGateway.com for one of their reading plans. Those nice folks over there email me a passage of Scripture to read every day, and it ends up taking me through the Bible in a year. It's the only way of reading Scripture I've ever been consistent with in my whole life.

I have friends who listen to Scripture out loud while they're driving. Some read the Bible around the table with their families at meal times. My parents end their day by reading a few verses out loud before they go to sleep. Many people like to write verses on notecards and stick them all over the house or in their purses.

God created you, and he knows how you learn best. He's not going to be offended if you approach Scripture in a way that makes sense with who you are. Ask him to give you insight into how you best eat of his Word, and then make sure you stay full.

## Have Conversations with God

Many of us learn prayer as children at the dinner table. We fold our hands, bow our heads, speak simple words.

It's a beautiful way to start.

And yet as an adult I struggle with prayer sometimes. My mind races. Distractions steal my focus. Good intentions turn to words unsaid.

Here's another confession: sometimes prayer feels, well, routine.

Ack! I can't believe I wrote that. But it's true.

Obviously, the problem isn't with the God of the universe. He's endlessly compelling and interesting. It will take all of eternity to know him.

So the only other logical conclusion is that the boring part is somewhere on my end. I thought I just needed to grin and bear it. But a co-worker recently loaned me a book called *Praying in Color: Drawing a New Path to God*.

The author, Sybil MacBeth, shares how she turned doodling into a form of focused prayer. Having recently purchased an unlined journal (my first!), I've found it freeing to write without lines. Now I've discovered I can pray without "lines" too.

Those lines aren't literal; they just represent all the "rules" that are often associated with prayer. Depending on where we grew up or what churches we've attended, they vary. But they usually cover things like how long we should pray, what words we should use, and the location or time or method.

I discovered that while those "lines" help many people (and if that's you, then hang on to them), for me they were really just artificial borders keeping me from experiencing God in more intimate ways.

David wrote psalms. Jesus spent time in the wilderness in prayer. Hannah made a trip to the temple. Paul prayed without ceasing.

God is endless and creative. Why shouldn't our communication with him be too?

## Find a New Way to Focus

I have a confession to make. (By the way, it seems like I confess to you a lot, doesn't it?) Anyway, here it goes: I'm a writer who doesn't keep a real, live, after-I-die-they'll-publish-it journal. Nope, I haven't done that since I was a freshman in college, and I hope no one ever finds that one. I may burn it. But that's another story.

My journaling consists of three things: me, my iPhone, and a little app called MyJournal. It lets me quickly write little notes wherever I am and even upload photos from my camera to go with them. Stay with me, it's going to get better. I began this type of journaling a little while ago. Before then I had tried to keep a journal but somehow it never became consistent and included a lot of whining.

One day it seemed as if God put the idea in my heart to start keeping a "good things" journal. This journal would include little blessings, encouraging words people shared with me, and other ways he showed his love in my life every day.

So I did it. At first it felt awkward. I felt prideful and a bit cheesy. But over time it started to rock my world because it made me realize how much I dwell on the negative. I would sit down at my keyboard and think, "What a rough day!" Then by the end of journaling, I would realize four or five really amazing things had happened.

I often tell my counseling clients our minds are like cars. If you let go of the steering wheel in your car, it will naturally drift one way or another. We're like that too. I think we all have a natural tendency to drift toward being negative. At least I do.

Because of that it's really important for me to do things, like my journal, that are the equivalent of me taking back the wheel. Well, it's really Jesus taking the wheel. (And we all know that song. Sing it with me now.)

### 7 Steps to Keeping a "Good Things" Journal

1. *Choose a time to journal each day. I do it right before bed. You need only five to ten minutes. If you miss a day (or three), give yourself grace.*
2. *Sit down in a quiet place with your journal or laptop. I prefer something electronic, but I do still have zillions of paper journals just because they make me happy.*

3. *Ask God to help you see through his eyes. Then start mentally digging through your day from beginning to end like a treasure hunter.*

4. *When something comes to mind, write one or two sentences about it in your journal. For example, "I had lunch with my dear friend, and we laughed so hard we almost fell out of our chairs. Thank you, God, for the gift of friendship."*

5. *If someone has spoken or written encouraging words to you that day, record those in your journal too.*

6. *Include short prayers (see #4) expressing gratitude.*

7. *Reread often, especially on hard days.*

That's it. I did mine the first year with a bit of reluctance. But when I sat down and reread it on January 1 of the following year, I was really hooked. I had forgotten about 80 percent of the blessings in my life, and I knew I'd probably do it again unless I kept going. (You're probably more spiritual than I am and would never do such a thing.)

You can do your journal however you'd like. It can be short or long. You can write in it daily, weekly, monthly, or whatever.

If you'd like to keep a gratitude journal, you might consider joining in with the community at *A Holy Experience* (http://www.aholyexperience.com/category/gratitude/).

All of the above are just ideas. Feel free to explore and figure out what works best for you. If you don't like journaling, don't do it. Go for a walk instead, or have a weekly coffee date with a truth-speaking friend. Whatever it looks like for you, it's all about pausing to see things differently. Because every time you do, you're teaching your brain to think differently too.

# Your Future Is Full of Hope

It's moments like these when I wish we weren't separated by pages. I'd love to go shopping with you for a new journal. Or help you write Scriptures on pretty notecards to place around your house (although you might not want that—my handwriting is terrible!). Or simply sit on the sofa and pray for a while about whatever it is that concerns you.

I want to whisper, "I know this isn't easy." You've made it this far, and that tells me so much about you—that you are a brave, beautiful, faithful woman. You are trying to trust even when you're not sure what's ahead. You're persevering when it would be easier to give up.

*I don't know what your future holds. But I know who holds you.*

I pray he shows you more of who he is and more of who you are in ways you never expected . . . and beyond what you've even dared to hope.

The news ticker for your life still reads, "Good things coming."

# 10

## You Really Are Going to Be **Okay**

We've come a long way together in the last few pages, friend. Thank you for sticking with me. Thank you for being brave, strong, and willing to think about your life and circumstances differently. Thank you for daring to decide that you really are going to be okay.

Whatever hard circumstance you're facing now, it's not likely to be the last one. As long as we dwell this side of heaven, we're going to face challenges from time to time and stress quite often. That's why I'm so passionate about the message of this book. Because what you've learned here isn't just for now; it's for always. I want to see you be a woman who lives with strength, joy, and most of all, resilience.

I love the word *resilience*. It means that you're able to thrive not just where you are now but for the rest of your life. It means not only can you handle the next step but you can finish well. It means that when you get home to heaven you will hear the words, "Well done, good and faithful servant."

In his book *A Resilient Life*, Gordon MacDonald says, "Too many people see life as a sprint—something fast, furious, quickly finished, bereft of any deep breathing. But life is more than a burst of speed. It is a distance run, and it demands endurance, determination, and a kick at the finish."[1]

You are not a sprinter. You are called to the race of life for the long haul.

> Therefore, since we are surrounded by such a great cloud of witnesses, let us throw off everything that hinders and the sin that so easily entangles. And let us run with perseverance the race marked out for us, fixing our eyes on Jesus, the pioneer and perfecter of faith. For the joy set before him he endured the cross, scorning its shame, and sat down at the right hand of the throne of God. Consider him who endured such opposition from sinners, so that you will not grow weary and lose heart. (Heb. 12:1–3)

That's true whether God grants you fifteen, fifty, or even a hundred years on this planet. You can run your race well. You can finish with hope. You can even dare to enjoy the journey.

Resilience doesn't come naturally to us. We're more likely to tire out and give up. Just look around you. How many people do you see who are *truly* living? You may think those who are have extraordinary genetics or a lot of luck. But I believe that resilience is always a choice—and it's always available to us.

## What Makes Someone Resilient?

I have a grandfather who is ninety-one years old at the time I'm writing these words. He just had a pacemaker put in last week. I talked to him yesterday, and he said he's looking forward to going to the beach this weekend. He's planning on traveling to the Gideons International convention in Dallas this July. He's still a greeter at his church. I asked him how he was doing after his procedure, and he said, "Well, I'm doing okay. I could be better. But I'm going to focus on what I've got."

## Choosing Your Attitude

In the statement above, my grandpa reflected one of the key characteristics of resilient people. They choose to focus on the positive in life. My grandpa has other similar sayings. For example, when I share that I'm worried about something, his reply is more often than not, "Well, just put it on the back burner of the stove and turn the heat off." In other words, don't focus on it or fuel it.

Don't misunderstand—my grandpa hasn't had an easy-breezy life. He's faced numerous health challenges in the last few years, he lost his wife of over fifty years, and the rest of his life hasn't been a walk in the park all the time either. But he has tenaciously decided that he will look on the bright side.

The authors of *What Happy Women Know* say, "Research suggests that optimists live longer, happier, and more satisfying lives."[2] They also have more good news to share. It turns out optimism can be *learned*.

I remember standing in my grandfather's home office one afternoon and reading the book titles on his shelves. A surprising number were what we would consider classics on positive thinking and faith. It became clear to me that at some point many years ago my grandpa had *decided* to live this way. He had made an intentional choice to approach life differently. And decades later it has paid off in ways that he probably never could have imagined.

Much of what we've talked through in this book is intended to equip you to make that decision too. Only you control your attitude and outlook. I've come to believe that optimism is essential to finishing the race of life well. And by optimism I don't mean a Pollyanna approach but rather a deep, abiding faith that God is good and he really will work out his best for us no matter what. Let's explore the specific ways we can express that faith in our lives.

## Staying in Your Strengths

For several decades my grandfather ran a Christian bookstore with my grandmother. Before that, he had his own paint store and at one point a gas station as well. He once remarked, "I've only worked for someone else one time—and that was in the Air Force." That approach to life makes sense for my grandpa because he's a gifted entrepreneur who has a talent for connecting with people. For the majority of his life, he's done most what he does best.

It turns out that's a key to resilience. We are each wired by God to fulfill a specific purpose in this world. He gave us strengths, skills, and specific people to serve. When we are doing so, we experience deep fulfillment. When we move away from that (even without realizing it), we find our energy and joy beginning to fade.

My internet connection becomes weaker the farther away from my wireless router I go. In many ways, our hearts are the same. The farther away we get from who God intended us to be, the weaker and more disconnected we feel.

And here's a shocking truth that's related to staying in your strengths: women today are not happier. Study after study shows that overall our gender has experienced a decrease in life satisfaction. That can be attributed to a number of factors, but one in particular stands out. Because we have so many choices and opportunities, ironically many of us are actually doing *less* of what we really love.

Think back over your last week, month, or year. When did you feel most alive? At what times did you sense God using you? How did you experience joy? Try to narrow that down to one instance in particular.

If nothing comes to mind, that's a warning sign. You are made to live in your strengths. You are made to live in the center of who God made you to be. If you're not, it doesn't mean you're failing, but it does mean that somewhere deep inside there is an SOS being sent out that you're not fully hearing. It's time to make changes. (If you're not sure how to do so, my book *You're Already Amazing* provides simple ways to find out who you are and what you're called to do.)

When stress, bad days, and hard times hit us, it's ironically our strengths and what brings us joy that are often the first to go.

We love writing and know we have a gift for it, but suddenly we can never find time to put words on a page.

We enjoy having friends over for dessert, but life gets so crazy that our gift of hospitality is stashed away in our closet along with our pretty cookie tray.

We thrive on helping those in need, but we hit a crisis and decide we're too messy to have anything to offer.

It's easy to do so. After all, we promise ourselves, "When things settle down and life gets back to normal, that will be the first thing I get back to again." But here's the thing: life doesn't get back to normal. There's always one more challenge to handle, another milestone to pass, a busy season to "just get through" again.

We have to fight hard to hold on to what we know God has placed us in this world to do. And that is not a selfish choice. Because what he's created us to do brings us so much joy, it can feel self-serving to pursue it when there seem to be so many other "needs" in our lives right now. But being who you are truly made to be is one of the greatest gifts you can offer others, God, and yourself.

Yes, in times of stress it may look different. You might need to make adjustments. You could be doing less than what you did before or pursuing it in a totally new way. But the point is, *don't let go.*

Don't let go of your strengths.

Don't let go of your skills.

Don't let go of who God has made you to be.

Marcus Buckingham, author of *Find Your Strongest Life*, says it this way:

> Life may ask everything of you, but you cannot do everything. You must learn how to choose, how to focus your life toward specific moments. You must learn how to create more of the strong-moments you want and how to celebrate the ones you have. Yours will not be a balanced life—as we'll see, balance is both impossible to maintain and unfulfilling on those few occasions when you do strike it. But if you learn to create and celebrate your strong-moments, yours will be a full life, inclined, tilted, targeted toward your strongest moments. So often you are told: "You must learn to say 'No.'" But, to live your strongest life, you must do the opposite. You must learn to say "Yes."[3]

You get to choose how to spend your life. God doesn't have a plan B for you. Being who you are not only makes you resilient—it also changes the world.

## Spending Your Life on Love

A little over a year ago, my grandpa had a ninetieth birthday party. I had the privilege of being there and serving punch. That put me in a position to do a lot of listening. Over fifty people packed into his house, and each one came with a story.

"I was in your grandpa's Sunday school class forty years ago."

"I used to shop in your grandpa's bookstore, and he always encouraged me."

"I'm in the Gideons with your grandpa. We've been friends for decades!"

"I go to your grandpa's church, and he hugs me every Sunday."

"I'm your grandpa's neighbor, and he makes me laugh whenever I see him."

On and on the stories went of how my grandpa has spent his life loving well, in little and big ways. I nodded my head in agreement because I've experienced the same. For over fifteen years now, my grandpa has taken me out on breakfast dates to ask me how I'm doing and encourage me in my faith.

My grandpa never went to Hollywood. He's not a CEO of a big corporation or a high-position politician. He's a regular guy in a small town who simply says yes when God asks to use him.

It turns out that doing so is not only a blessing to those around him; it's also probably one of the reasons he's lived so long. Research has shown that those who have strong relationships and serve others tend to live healthier, more joyful lives.

When we go through stress, it's easy to hunker down and withdraw from others. I certainly tend to respond that way. If I'm having a hard day, I'm more likely to sit on the corner of the couch with some chocolate for a private pity party than to reach out to those around me. I'm slowly learning that choice isn't beneficial.

We are made to connect with others. Daniel Goleman, author of *Social Intelligence*, says, "Our brain has been preset for kindness."[4] He goes on to share that we are always impacted by those around us. Through brain "loops" we catch each other's moods like colds. Watch two friends having an intimate conversation. Their body language almost always synchronizes without them even realizing it. What this ultimately means is that when we bring joy to others, it comes back to us in both spiritual and physical ways.

When we're stressed, we need to shift our internal state, and serving others can be one of the most effective ways to do so. Ironically, when we need it most is often when we're likely to do this least. That can be due to lower energy (and sometimes what we really do need is simply rest). But I think it can also be because of a lie that we believe: "I have to have it all together before I can help someone else."

Have you ever felt this way? I have. But it's simply not true. Throughout Scripture God uses messy, broken people right in the middle of their greatest challenges. We don't need to have it all together. Wherever we are today, we can serve in some way. Even if it's just offering a smile to the nurse in our hospital room. Or making our toddler giggle when we're almost at the end of our patience. Or listening to a friend at church on Sunday morning when we'd really like to get home to our house and the couch instead.

What I've seen through my grandpa's life is that true service isn't about grand gestures; it's about a series of small choices. Most of them unseen. Many we won't know the impact of this side of heaven. All of which add up to a lifetime of resilience and loving well.

## Changing and Growing

My grandpa and I talk on the phone every Sunday. When I ask him how he's doing, his reply is usually the same: "Well, I got up this morning!" Then we both laugh together.

What he really means is that he takes life one day at a time. It turns out that's a helpful approach, especially when we want to see change happen. When we'd like things to be different, we tend to think in big terms. We'll get a new job. Go to another city. Find someone to marry.

But change and growth actually only happen one little bit at a time.

The trouble with thinking in small and immediate terms is that we tend to see so many obstacles right in front of us. How do we see around them to start envisioning how things can be different?

Solution-focused therapy, the type of counseling I'm trained in, often uses a simple technique to start down that path. It's a little exercise called "The Miracle Question." When a counselor uses this question in therapy, they ask something like this:

> Imagine that when you go home tonight, a miracle takes place and the problem that brought you to therapy completely disappears. But of course, since it was a miracle, you don't know it has happened. What will be the first thing you notice the next day that will tell you it has happened?[5]

Research has shown this to be a powerful and effective tool in helping people move past obstacles. That question is followed by more questions that open the door for details: What's the first thing you would do that day? How are you feeling? Who are you with? What are you wearing? And then what happens?

After you process through the whole day, it's time to take a look at how to turn what you've discovered into actual realistic steps. For example, a woman might say, "I would wake up and my cancer would be gone. Then I would have breakfast out with my girlfriends! I haven't done that in months." The counselor might say, "It sounds like you're really missing spending time with friends. How can you do that now?" Then together the counselor and client would come up with ideas, such as her friends bringing breakfast to her house.

Even with something unchangeable, like the loss of a loved one, going through the miracle question can help someone start identifying what they're missing most. That opens the door to thinking about getting needs met in new ways. Of course, there will still be grief along the way, and it won't be easy. Yet this exercise does help people begin the valuable process of moving forward even in the toughest situations.

I love this technique because anyone can do it. It taps into your imagination, creativity, and ability to come up with solutions.

· · · · · · · · · · · · · **The Miracle Question** · · · · · · · · · · · · ·

*Imagine that when you go home tonight, a miracle takes place and the problem that brought you to therapy completely disappears. But of course, since it was a miracle, you don't know it has happened. What will be the first thing you notice the next day that will tell you it has happened?*

---

---

---

*What will be the next thing you notice after that?*

---

---

*What will you do differently that day?*

---

---

---

*How will you feel different?*

_____

_____

_____

*Who will be with you?*

_____

_____

_____

*What will you be thinking as you drift off to sleep that night?*

_____

_____

_____

*What did you learn about what you really want based on the day you described? Given your current reality, what are some creative ways to make some of that happen in spite of your circumstances?*

_____

_____

_____

You are more resourceful than you might think. Adapting to life simply means remaining open and being willing to try new things. You've done that again and again throughout your life—most of the time without even realizing it. How will tomorrow be different for you?

## Redefining Success

I slip out of my bed and shuffle into the kitchen. My grandpa is already there with a Bible in his hands. He looks up from his reading. "Good morning, H.E.!" (That's my nickname because I'm actually named after him. He's Hollie. I'm Holley.) He asks if I want coffee, and I nod yes as I drowsily make my way to the pot to start some for both of us. As I do, I watch him continue reading. He's done this for as long as I can remember. For my grandpa, Scripture isn't a religious text. It's a guide. Most of all, it keeps him focused on what a life well lived really means.

It's a question we all want answered: What is success, really?

We have so many choices about how to spend our lives.

We can climb the corporate ladder.

We can try to raise the perfect family.

We can move overseas and become missionaries.

How do we know what's really best? Even when we think we know, where we often end up leaves us feeling hollow. Or life circumstances make it clear that the dream we defined as "success" isn't going to happen in the way we imagined.

What then?

I found myself on that search a few years ago. I'd come through a very difficult personal season. It was followed by another one full of answered prayers and joy. Yet even seeing so many hopes become reality didn't fill me up on the inside the way I imagined it would. It didn't really feel like success.

So I decided to go to the same place I had seen my grandpa turn to many times. I flipped open the pages of my Bible and said, "God, I need to know what success really means."

I found the answer in this verse in Matthew: "His lord said to him, 'Well done, good and faithful servant; you were faithful over a few things, I will make you ruler over many things. Enter into the joy of your lord'" (25:21 NKJV).

I'd read these sentences many times before. I imagine you have too. What stood out to me this time was one little phrase: "*enter into* the joy of your lord."

I realized in that moment that God's joy in us doesn't begin when we get to heaven. We can live in a way that brings him joy *now*.

That is success, friend.

*Being a servant who brings joy to your master.*

Here's the beautiful reality that comes with that truth: nothing can stop you from being successful. You can bring God joy in the corner office or in a hospital room. You can bring him joy changing diapers or changing a church. You can bring God joy when you're young and when you're nearing the end of your life.

And here's more good news: you never have to compete with or be compared to anyone.

*We all have an equal capacity to bring God joy.*

Stress and difficulties don't diminish that capacity. You can bring God joy anytime, anywhere, through anything, and nothing can change that reality.

To put it simply, *love God and you cannot fail.* No matter what. Isn't that extraordinary?

So what exactly brings our Master joy? It's not a long list of rules and requirements. It's not being the biggest and best in the eyes of the world. It's not about experience, education, or making the right impression. It's simply this: "'Love the Lord your God with all your heart and with all your soul and with all your mind.' This is the first and greatest commandment. And the second is like it: 'Love your neighbor as yourself'" (Matt. 22:37–39).

It all comes back to love. And love always begins with receiving first. "We love because he first loved us" (1 John 4:19).

You don't have to try harder, do more, get better. You only need to receive God's love and then respond.

That's success.

At my grandpa's party, my thoughts drifted toward heaven. With each hug and encouraging word I watched him receive, I imagined how many more he'll get when he's home forever. That's where a lifetime of love leads us.

The same can be true of you, friend.

Simply love. Wherever you are today, with whatever you have to offer, love and you'll bring greater joy to your Master and fellow servants than you could ever even know this side of eternity.

## Handling Life's Ups and Downs

In a few days, I'll leave to visit my grandpa Hollie. We'll sit around his breakfast table to drink coffee and tell stories. He'll tease me mercilessly. We'll spend some time at South Padre Island near his house as well.

I've gone to that beach as long as I can remember. I've jumped in its waves and picked up shells on the shore. I've gone fishing in its waters and gotten a pretty good sunburn a few times too. I feel at home near the ocean.

Every time I go there now, I think of some wise words my friend and boss for many years, Linn Carlson, once offered me. I found myself going through a difficult time and he said, "Holley,

I've found that life is a lot like the waves. There are always ups and downs."

At the time, I was in my early twenties, and I still had the unrealistic notion that at some point I could sustain the "up" forever. Stress and challenges kept catching me off guard, like a stray wave crashing into my back at the beach. I tucked Linn's words into my heart, and I still pull them out from time to time. Just this week I found myself feeling a little down for no apparent reason. "Just ride out the wave," I whispered to myself. "It will get better." And eventually it did.

I realize some waves are deeper and stronger and longer than others. Some feel more like a tsunami. But even in those, I believe God promises that we will not be overwhelmed and they will not last forever.

Sometimes, like Peter, we even get to walk on water.

I remember talking with a friend who said, "I think another wave is coming your way! Now is the time to get ready." I tucked those words away in my heart too and wondered, "Then how do I prepare so I can walk on water with Jesus when it comes?"

As I prayed about that one morning, it seemed God whispered to my heart to turn to chapter 4 of a book I'd just received. How did the chapter begin? With a story about a huge wave that hit Asia and the plans being made to ensure a better outcome in the future.

One phrase leaped out: get to higher ground. It echoed in my heart because ever since the new year started, I've also been asking God to teach me to live in joy—which is the higher ground of the heart.

All kinds of waves come into our lives. They can flow from a tide of blessings or come out of a storm. Happy or hard, they can overwhelm us if we end up treading water in our own strength (not that I know from experience—ahem).

I wondered, "Okay, God, how do I get my heart to higher ground so I'm ready? Where do you want me to go?"

The next morning I read a verse in Psalms about joy. I loved it so much that I wrote it in my journal:

> But let all who take refuge in you be glad;
>> let them ever sing for joy.
> Spread your protection over them,
>> that those who love your name may rejoice in you.
> Surely, Lord, you bless the righteous;
>> you surround them with your favor as with a shield.
> (Ps. 5:11–12)

I loved the imagery of the verse—how it says God not only spreads his protection over us but also surrounds us on every side. I even drew a picture of it in my journal and wrote the phrase "like the cleft in the rock."

You remember the story about the cleft in the rock, don't you? The Israelites are on their way to the Promised Land. They rebel and God says he'll no longer go with them. Moses begs for God's mercy and says they won't go to higher ground without him:

> Moses said to him, "If your Presence does not go with us, do not send us up from here." . . . The Lord said to Moses, "I will do the very thing you have asked." . . . Then Moses said, "Now show me your glory." . . . Then the Lord said, "There is a place near me where you may stand on a rock. When my glory passes by, I will put you in a cleft in the rock and cover you with my hand until I have passed by." (Exod. 33:15, 17–18, 21–22)

A few days later on a quiet morning, I opened Sheila Walsh's new book *The Shelter of God's Promises*. In the first few pages, she shares a story of going to higher ground. This time it's quite literal—a hiking trip to the mountains with friends during college. Through some hilarious as well as anxiety-producing circumstances, Sheila winds up spending the night in a cave, and God uses that experience to show her he is her true shelter. She closes this chapter, which encapsulates the heart of the book, with these words:

> What has had the most lasting impact on me is that, in the storm and under pressure, God took me to a place of rest, comfort, and ultimately, to a place of absolute beauty. Even among discomfort, disappointment, and displacement, I was kept safe.
>
> From a cleft in a rock, a new day dawned, a glimpse of splendor and glory, and a moment of such beautiful fellowship with God that I knew he loved me deeply, intimately, surely, as sure as the rock I stood upon.[6]

Sheila made her way to higher ground on that hiking trip. She found the shelter her heart needed not just for that night but for all of life. And it wasn't just a place—it was a Person. I thought back to the questions I'd asked: "God, how do I get my heart to higher ground? Where do you want me to go?"

To the cleft in the rock.

To Christ.

The One who will shelter us—*no matter what may come.*

The One who will walk on water with us—*yes, the time will come!*

Are you ready to move onward and upward together, friend?

## Finishing Well

I wish I could introduce you to my grandpa Hollie. He'd shake your hand and hug your neck (he insists three hugs a day makes you live longer). He'd even go out with us for coffee or tea and a big piece of pie.

Then we'd both listen to you and your story. What you're facing now, what you've been through, how God has been faithful in unexpected ways through it all.

My grandpa would probably say to you what he does to me: "Hang in there." I've learned what he really means by "hang in there" is more like "hold on."

Hold on to hope.

Hold on to who you are.

Hold on to all God has promised.

That's what I want to say to you too. No matter what you're facing, no matter how hard it seems, no matter how much you feel like giving up on some days, *hold on.*

You're going to be okay.

Not because life is easy.

Not because you have it all together.

Not because everything will work out the way you want.

You're going to make it through this because of *who you are and who you belong to.*

You are a woman of strength. You are a daughter of the King. You are made for a Promised Land.

I'm so glad we got to share this part of the journey together. I'll be thinking of you and praying for you. Will you do the same for me?

Whatever life brings our way, we can handle it together.

And one day we'll be Home.

We'll be with the One we love forever.

Then we'll hear those words we've longed for all our lives: "Well done, good and faithful servant; you were faithful over a few things, I will make you ruler over many things. Enter into the joy of your lord'" (Matt. 25:21 NKJV).

..............

Can you hear the whisper of it even now?
Lean in close and listen one more time to what's true . . .
You are a woman who's loved.
You are a woman who brings joy.
*You are a woman who's really going to be okay.*

# Go Deeper Guide
## (for Individuals and Groups)

You can download a free printable version of this guide on the Books & More page at www.holleygerth.com.

## Chapter 1: Who You Are Is Still the Same

1. What's the best thing going on in your life right now? What's the hardest?

2. What are the words you have been using to describe who you are based on where you are in life right now? Write three here (for example, *stressed, divorced, sick, lonely*):

3. To help shift your perspective, rewrite those words as phrases that show they aren't part of your identity. For example, "I'm going through a stressful time right now" or "I have experienced a divorce" or "I'm battling an illness."

4. What's one truth about who God says you are that you need to remember today?

5. We sometimes struggle to believe we're really loved by God. We think his love is conditional and has to be earned. How would you fill in this sentence? "If I am _____ (e.g., perfect) then I am loved. So if _____ (e.g., I'm broken) then I must not be loved."

6. Read Romans 8:38–39. How does this change what you wrote for the last question? What does God say to you instead?

7. Just before the passage above, Paul reassures us that our difficulties can't cause us to be condemned and that we will ultimately have victory. Read Romans 8:33–37. Personalize this passage by filling in this sentence:

> "In all these things, even in _____ (write your biggest struggle right now), I am more than a conqueror through him who loved me."

8. What else did God whisper to your heart as you read these pages? What's one small way you'll apply what you've learned?

_____

_____

_____

## Chapter 2: You're Stronger Than You Know

1. What circumstantial strength(s) did you circle on the list in this chapter?

_____

_____

_____

2. Think for a moment about the last time you let yourself slip into a downward spiral. What led to it? If you could go back, what would you do differently? What circumstantial strengths would you ask God to give you instead?

_____

_____

_____

3. Think again to the last hard day you had. What is one thing you did well despite everything that was going on?

_____

_____

_____

4. Who supports and encourages you in stressful times? How do they do so?

5. God uses your life education. What's one lesson you've learned in life that would be helpful to you right now?

6. God uses your life experiences. What's something you've gone through in life that can help you with the stress and circumstances you're facing today?

7. Which name of God spoke most deeply to your heart? Why?

8. What else did God whisper to your heart as you read these pages? What's one small way you'll apply what you've learned?

# Chapter 3: Your Mind Is a Powerful Gift

1. God has physically created us in extraordinary ways. What's one new thing you learned about how your brain works?

2. Review the four stages of change and then think of an area of your life in which you have experienced change. Describe your process of going through the four stages.

3. Which short-term strategy spoke to you most? How will you try it this week?

4. What kind of processor are you? What do you usually need to think through things (such as time alone, conversation with a friend, or reading Scriptures on the topic)?

5. What are some ways or times you pray? When do you feel closest to God and what helps you do so?

6. Read Philippians 4:8. Which "whatever" do you need most right now and for what situation in your life?

7. What is a thought you have been battling this week? What truth does God want to replace it with instead?

8. What else did God whisper to your heart as you read these pages? What's one small way you'll apply what you've learned?

## Chapter 4: Your Heart Is Worth Guarding

1. Read Proverbs 4:23. What does it mean to you to "guard your heart"?

2. What are some of the emotions you've experienced this week (see the chart in this chapter if you need ideas, and choose at least one)? How did you express those emotions?

_____

_____

3. Practice going through this process:

I am feeling:

_____

Because (first thing that comes to mind):

_____

Is this really the reason? If yes, then continue.
If no, then write a new reason:

_____

What do I need right now?

_____

What's the first small thing I am going to do about that need?

_____

What truth do I need to believe in this moment?

_____

4. Besides "one another" relationships, which type are you most likely to be in?

_____

_____

5. Which "one another" characteristic spoke to you most? Share an example from your life of seeing it in action.

6. Who is on the throne of your life right now? What are some ways you can tell when it's Jesus and when it's you?

7. Describe a situation when you guarded your heart. What did you do and how did that protect you in some way?

8. What else did God whisper to your heart as you read these pages? What's one small way you'll apply what you've learned?

## Chapter 5: You Can Keep from Sabotaging Yourself

1. Read Romans 7:15–24. Can you relate to what Paul shares? What phrase that he uses do you identify with most?

2. What's one expectation you've been trying to fulfill? What is the invitation God wants to replace it with instead?

3. Think about what your signature insecurity might be.

   What was the last situation you were in when you felt insecure?

   What were you afraid would happen?

   Why would it matter to you if that did happen?

   The answer to the third question probably gives you a glimpse into a core part of who you are, what you value, and how God uses you. *We are most vulnerable to insecurity in those places.*

4. Based on the answers to the questions above, what do you think your signature insecurity might be?

   My signature insecurity is:

   When that button gets pushed, I usually react this way:

   With God's help I'm going to try to respond like this instead:

5. What is the difference between guilt and conviction?

6. What are you doing to take care of your body right now? What helps you feel your best?

7. Which area are you thriving in most right now (social, emotional, spiritual, physical)? Which one is your biggest struggle, and what kind of support do you need in it?

8. What else did God whisper to your heart as you read these pages? What's one small way you'll apply what you've learned?

## Chapter 6: You're Made for a Promised Land

1. Read the three Scripture passages at the beginning of this chapter. What do they have in common?

2. Think of a time in your life when you passed through a difficulty. How did God bring you to the other side?

3. Which of the myths resonated with you most?

4. When you read the ways to get unstuck, was there one that you need now or that you have used in the past?

5. Think of an area of your life where you are making choices right now. Where would you place it on the chart?

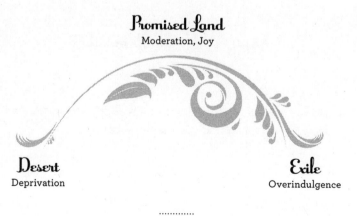

**Promised Land**
Moderation, Joy

**Desert**
Deprivation

**Exile**
Overindulgence

6. What's one step you can take toward the Promised Land? Or if you're already there, what will help you stay there?

7. What helps you "fight for joy" even on hard days?

8. Fill in this blank: I'm not going to settle for

9. What else did God whisper to your heart as you read these pages? What's one small way you'll apply what you've learned?

## Chapter 7: You'll Remember These Words

1. Do you ever feel unseen or wonder if what you do is noticed? How does God remind you that he sees you?

2. Where do you tend to find your worth? What helps you receive it from God?

3. Have you ever worried that something in your past or a struggle you're facing right now could disqualify you from being used by God? What is it and what's the truth?

4. Have you ever felt like quitting? How did God give you the strength to keep going?

5. Is it hard for you to celebrate when you're stressed or something difficult is happening? What's a small way to do so?

6. What does "rest" mean to you? How do you receive it from God and incorporate it into your life?

7. What are you most looking forward to in heaven?

8. Read the Scriptures on the last page of this chapter. What else did God whisper to your heart as you read these pages? What's one small way you'll apply what you've learned?

_____

_____

_____

## Chapter 8: You Can Make the Most of Change

1. What changes are you experiencing in your life right now? Are they anticipated or unanticipated?

_____

_____

_____

2. Read Genesis 1:28. Then review the "What's within Our Boundaries?" list. Which of these is easiest for you to take charge of? Which one is most difficult?

_____

_____

_____

3. What else do you wish was under your control? How can you release that to God?

_____

_____

4. What does God want you to do about this change in your life?

5. What are the best uses of your emotions and energy right now? What will your top three priorities be in this time of change?

6. What in your life do you need help with or to release while you're working through this change?

7. Describe some changes you've already been through in life. What helped you get through those that might apply now?

8. What else did God whisper to your heart as you read these pages? What's one small way you'll apply what you've learned?

# Chapter 9: Your Future Is Full of Hope

1. What do you tend to worry about most?

2. Read Matthew 6:25-34. What do you find most reassuring in what Jesus says?

3. How would you explain the difference between worry and wonder or concern?

4. In the section on who God is, which truth spoke the most deeply to your fears?

5. Think of a challenging situation in your life right now and then walk through these questions.

    Who is God showing himself to be in this situation? What is he revealing to you about his character?

What else do you need to know about him right now?
Ask him to show you.

_____

_____

How is who he is showing you more about who you are?
(For example, "Because God is always with me, I am
never alone.")

_____

_____

How do you want to become more like him through this
situation?

_____

_____

6. How do you help your brain focus on truth and have hope?
What appeals to you most about these ideas?

_____

_____

7. What do you need to release to God when it comes to your
fears about the future?

_____

_____

8. What else did God whisper to your heart as you read these
pages? What's one small way you'll apply what you've learned?

_____

_____

# Chapter 10: You Really Are Going to Be Okay

1. Read Hebrews 12:1–3. How would you define resilience? Who in your life is an example of resilience?

2. What helps you keep a positive attitude even in hard times? What's something new you've learned about that from this book?

3. What are some of your strengths, gifts, or skills? Which ones are you using most right now?

4. How do you show love to others? Who is showing love to you right now?

5. What's your definition of true success? What are your thoughts on the definition offered in this chapter?

6. Practice using "The Miracle Question."

> Imagine that when you go home tonight a miracle takes place and your problem completely disappears. But of course, being a miracle, you don't know it has happened. What will be the first thing you notice the next day that will tell you it has happened?

> What will be the next thing you notice?

> What will you do differently that day?

> How will you feel different?

> Who will be with you?

> What will you be thinking as you drift off to sleep that night?

> What did you learn about what you really want based on the day you described? Given your current reality, what are some creative ways to make some of that happen in spite of your circumstances?

7. What would you like people to say about you when you've gone to heaven?

_____

_____

_____

8. What else did God whisper to your heart as you read these pages? What's one small way you'll apply what you've learned?

_____

_____

_____

# Acknowledgments

*Thank you to my fantastic husband, Mark.* Your partnership, your friendship, and the life we share together bring me more joy than I can even express in words. You are, and always will be, one of God's greatest gifts to me.

*Thank you to my family* for their love, support, and prayers through the years. Dad, Mom, Granny Eula, and Poppi—I'm grateful for the legacy of faith you gave me growing up. And to the Gerths—I'm so glad I married into a family who loves Jesus and each other.

*Thank you to my friends* for loving me just as I am—for laughing with me, listening to my ideas, and giving me chocolate when I need it most. Kim, you get a special shout-out for traveling with me when I speak and being a steady encourager in so many ways.

I'm especially grateful for the women in my small group, the (in)courage girls, and the God-Sized Dream Team.

*Thank you to my publishing team* for being fantastic. I'm so grateful to Jennifer, Michele, Twila, Robin, and Wendy for all the ways you help my words get out there into the world (and for making sure they're at their best when they do).

*Thank you to DaySpring and (in)courage* for your support and partnering with me. Linn Carlson, I know you don't like getting compliments, but you can't delete this one, so I'm saying it—you have been one of God's best gifts to me, and I appreciate your friendship and leadership more than you will ever know.

*Thank you to my readers* for hanging out with me online at www.holleygerth.com as well as through the pages of my books. One of the things I'm most looking forward to in heaven is hugging each and every one of your necks!

*Most of all, thank you to Jesus* for letting me be your servant, daughter, and beloved. Use me as little or as much as you want. Success for me is bringing joy to you.

# Notes

## Introduction

1. "Fourteen Days to a Happier, Healthier You!" *Self*, March 2012, http://www.self.com/health/2012/03/14-days-to-happier-healthier-you-slideshow#slide=1.

## Chapter 1 Who You Are Is Still the Same

1. Jennifer Dukes Lee, email to the author, August 14, 2013. Used by permission.

2. Holley Gerth, *You're Already Amazing: Embracing Who You Are, Becoming All God Created You to Be* (Grand Rapids: Revell, 2012), 39.

## Chapter 2 You're Stronger Than You Know

1. Daily Mail Reporter, "'Supermothers' and Grandfather Lift 1 Ton Renault Clio Off Trapped Schoolboy," *Daily Mail*, June 4, 2009, http://www.dailymail.co.uk/news/article-1190759/Mighty-mothers-superhuman-strength-lift-1-400kg-car-run-schoolboy.html.

2. Janet Kornblum, "Study: 25% of Americans Have No One to Confide In," *USA Today*, June 22, 2006, www.usatoday.com/news/nation/2006-06-22-friendship_x.htm.

3. Kristen Welch, "When Nothing Is All You Have to Give," *(in)courage* (blog), June 4, 2012, http://www.incourage.me/2012/06/when-nothing-is-all-you-have-to-give.html.

4. Ann Voskamp, "Peace Is a Person," *A Holy Experience* (blog), October 29, 2007, http://www.aholyexperience.com/2007/10/peace-is-person.

## Chapter 3 Your Mind Is a Powerful Gift

1. Lisa-Jo Baker, "You're Right, Christian Women [and (in)courage Writers] Aren't Immune from Cliques," *(in)courage* (blog), June 5, 2012, http://www.incourage.me/2012/06/youre-right-christian-women-and-incourage-writers-arent-immune-from-cliques.html.

2. H. M. Tomlinson, "The Gift," in *Out of Soundings* (New York and London: Harper & Brothers Publishers, 1931), 148–59.

3. Laurel Mellin, *Wired for Joy: A Revolutionary Method for Creating Happiness from Within* (Carlsbad, CA: Hay House, 2010), 4.

4. Ibid., 7.

5. Lysa TerKeurst, *Unglued: Making Wise Choices in the Midst of Raw Emotions* (Grand Rapids: Zondervan, 2012), 14.

6. Gary Oliver, "Christian Foundations in Counseling," lecture, John Brown University, Siloam Springs, AR, 2007.

7. Mellin, *Wired for Joy*, 6–7.

## Chapter 4  Your Heart Is Worth Guarding

1. "Paul Ekman," Wikipedia, http://en.wikipedia.org/wiki/Paul_Ekman, modified August 3, 2013.

2. Pete Wilson, *Empty Promises: The Truth about You, Your Desires, and the Lies You're Believing* (Nashville: Thomas Nelson, 2012), 3.

## Chapter 5  You Can Keep from Sabotaging Yourself

1. Mark Seal, "The Devils in the Diva," *Vanity Fair*, June 2012, http://www.vanityfair.com/hollywood/2012/06/whitney-houston-death-bathtub-drugs-rehab.

2. Chris Crowley and Henry S. Lodge, MD, *Younger Next Year for Women: Live Strong, Fit, and Sexy until You're 80 and Beyond* (New York: Workman Publishing, 2010), 47.

3. Mayo Clinic Staff, "Depression and Anxiety: Exercise Eases Symptoms," Mayo Clinic, http://www.mayoclinic.com/health/depression-and-exercise/MH00043, accessed August 9, 2013.

## Chapter 6  You're Made for a Promised Land

1. Sonya Lyubormirskly, Kennon M. Sheldon, and David Schkade, "Pursuing Happiness: The Architecture of Sustainable Change," *Review of General Psychology* 9, no. 2 (2005): 111–31.

2. Gretchen Rubin, *The Happiness Project: Or, Why I Spent a Year Trying to Sing in the Morning, Clean My Closets, Fight Right, Read Aristotle, and Generally Have More Fun* (New York: HarperCollins, 2009), 215–16.

3. Sara Frankl, *Gitzen Girl* (blog), http://gitzengirl.blogspot.com/.

## Chapter 8  You Can Make the Most of Change

1. John Ortberg, *When the Game Is Over, It All Goes Back in the Box* (Grand Rapids: Zondervan, 2008), 78.

2. Ibid., 77.

3. Dr. Henry Cloud and Dr. John Townsend, *Boundaries: When to Say Yes, When to Say No to Take Control of Your Life* (Grand Rapids: Zondervan, 1992), 29.

4. Ibid., 40–48.

5. Quoted in Ortberg, *When the Game Is Over*, 80.

## Chapter 9  Your Future Is Full of Hope

1. Brené Brown, keynote speech (Blissdom blogging conference, Nashville, TN, January 27, 2011).

## Chapter 10  You Really Are Going to Be Okay

1. Gordon MacDonald, *A Resilient Life: You Can Move Ahead No Matter What* (Nashville: Thomas Nelson, 2004), 146.

2. Dan Baker, PhD, and Cathy Greenberg, PhD, with Ina Yalof, *What Happy Women Know: How New Findings in Positive Psychology Can Change Women's Lives for the Better* (New York: Rodale, 2007), 186.

3. Marcus Buckingham, *Find Your Strongest Life: What the Happiest and Most Successful Women Do Differently* (Nashville: Thomas Nelson, 2009), 94–95.

4. Daniel Goleman, *Social Intelligence: The New Science of Human Relationships* (New York: Bantam Dell, 2006), 60.

5. John Sharry, Brendan Madden, and Melissa Darmody, *Becoming a Solution Detective: Identifying Your Clients' Strengths in Practical Brief Therapy* (New York: The Haworth Clinical Practice Press, 2003), 30.

6. Sheila Walsh, *In the Shelter of God's Promises* (Nashville: Thomas Nelson, 2011), xvii.

# About Holley

Holley Gerth is a bestselling author who loves sharing God's heart for women through words. She does so through books like *You're Already Amazing* and through her partnership with DaySpring, as well as by being a life coach.

When she's not writing, Holley loves spending time with her husband, Mark, having coffee with girlfriends, and whipping up delicious things in the kitchen. She enjoys feeding people encouraging words and good food.

Holley would love to hang out with you at her place online (www.holleygerth.com). You can sign up for free email devotionals when you're there too.

**Look for Holley's other books from Revell:**
*You're Already Amazing*
*You're Made for a God-Sized Dream*
*The "Do What You Can" Plan* (ebook)
*Opening the Door to Your God-Sized Dream*
*If We Could Have Coffee . . .* (ebook)

Also find DaySpring cards and gifts from Holley at www.dayspring.com and in local Christian stores.

Holley donates a portion of her author proceeds to Compassion International's Leadership Development Program (www.compassion.com).

This ebook is the perfect companion to
*You're Going to Be Okay.*
So take a well-deserved break and have
a cup of coffee with a friend . . .

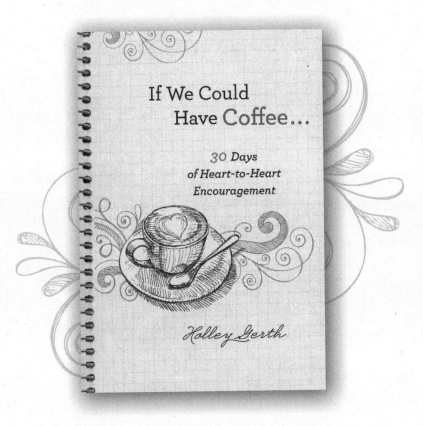

"Think of these words as little love notes for your life.
Love notes that started in the heart of God and just happen
to be delivered by me to you."

—*Holley Gerth*

# Discover the dreams God has given you—
## *and then dare to pursue them.*

Holley Gerth takes you by the heart and says,
"Yes! You can do this!" She guides you with insightful
questions, action plans to take the next steps, and most
of all, the loving hand of a friend.

# Take a 40-day journey with Holley Gerth
## *and discover your God-Sized Dream.*

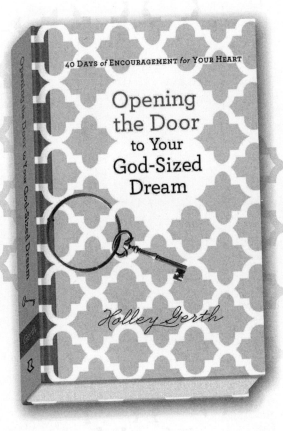

If you're ready to discover more about who you are and
the journey God has for you, you'll find the reassurance and
confidence you're looking for within these pages.

Revell
*a division of Baker Publishing Group*
www.RevellBooks.com

# This ebook is the perfect companion to Holley's *You're Made for a God-Sized Dream.*

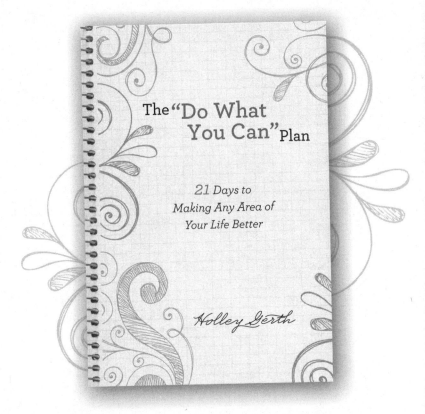

The "Do What You Can" Plan

*21 Days to Making Any Area of Your Life Better*

*Holley Gerth*

No matter what change you'd like to see in your life, you can make progress in just three weeks by taking new steps and overcoming the obstacles that have been getting in your way. Bestselling author and life coach Holley Gerth will be your partner on this journey. Her 21-day "Do What You Can" Plan guides you closer to God's best for you through encouraging Scriptures, personal stories, and practical action tools.

R Revell
a division of Baker Publishing Group
www.RevellBooks.com

"Holley Gerth turns words like a poet. Warm and personal, *You're Already Amazing* is a biblical, practical handbook for every woman's heart."

— Emily P. Freeman, author of *Grace for the Good Girl*

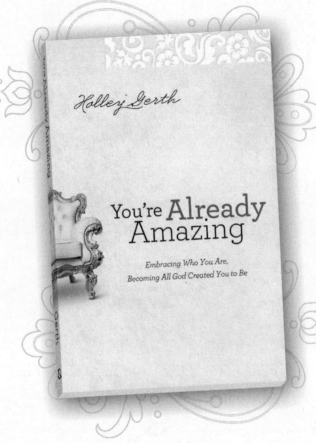

With this heart-to-heart message, Holley Gerth invites you to embrace one very important truth—that you truly are already amazing. Like a trusted friend, Holley gently shows you how to forget the lies and expectations the world feeds you and instead believe that God loves you and has bigger plans for your life than you've even imagined.

ℛ Revell
*a division of Baker Publishing Group*
www.RevellBooks.com

Available Wherever Books Are Sold
Also Available in Ebook Format